D0779729

Praise for *Designing for Performance*

"Designing for Performance *is the book to hand to anyone—designer or developer—who wants to start making faster sites. Lara carefully and clearly explains not just how you can create better performing sites, but how you can champion performance within your organization ensuring it remains a priority long after launch.*"

TIM KADLEC—INDEPENDENT DEVELOPER AND CONSULTANT

"*A web experience's performance evokes emotion from users just as much—if not more—than its aesthetics. Lara's book is so essential because she helps us understand that performance isn't just a technical best practice; it's an essential design consideration. By providing a slew of helpful tips and best practices, Lara provides a map for anyone looking to establish a culture of performance in their work.*"

BRAD FROST—WEB DESIGNER

"*Speed is an integral part of design. A beautiful website or app that takes forever to load will be viewed by no one. This book gives designers the knowledge they need to build fast web experiences.*"

JASON GRIGSBY—CO-FOUNDER, CLOUD FOUR

"*Design is the foundation of your performance strategy: it defines the user experience and expectations, shapes development, and directly impacts operations. This book should be required reading for designers and developers alike.*"

ILYA GRIGORIK—WEB PERFORMANCE ENGINEER, GOOGLE

"*If you've ever wondered how aesthetic choices impact performance or how cellular networks degrade your site's user experience, read this book.* Designing for Performance *gives you the tools to make and measure high impact performance improvements on your site, including actionable strategies to increase awareness of performance across your company. Great performance is good design.*"

JASON HUFF—PRODUCT DESIGN MANAGER, ETSY

Designing for Performance

Weighing Aesthetics and Speed

Lara Callender Hogan

 Beijing · Cambridge · Farnham · Köln · Sebastopol · Tokyo

Designing for Performance
by Lara Callender Hogan

Copyright © 2015 Lara Callender Hogan. All rights reserved.
Printed in Canada.

Published by O'Reilly Media, Inc.,
1005 Gravenstein Highway North, Sebastopol, CA 95472.

O'Reilly books may be purchased for educational, business, or sales promotional use. Online editions are also available for most titles (*https://www.safaribooksonline.com/*). For more information, contact our corporate/institutional sales department: (800) 998-9938 or *corporate@oreilly.com*.

Editors: Mary Treseler and Angela Rufino
Production Editor: Kara Ebrahim
Copyeditor: Rachel Monaghan
Proofreader: Charles Roumeliotis
Indexer: Ginny Munroe

Cover Designer: Ellie Volckhausen
Interior Designers: Ron Bilodeau and Monica Kamsvaag
Illustrator: Rebecca Demarest
Compositor: Kara Ebrahim

December 2014: First Edition.

Revision History for the First Edition:

2014-11-20   First release

See *http://www.oreilly.com/catalog/errata.csp?isbn=0636920033578* for release details.

The O'Reilly logo is a registered trademark of O'Reilly Media, Inc. *Designing for Performance*, the cover image, and related trade dress are trademarks of O'Reilly Media, Inc.

While the publisher and the author have used good faith efforts to ensure that the information and instructions contained in this work are accurate, the publisher and the author disclaim all responsibility for errors or omissions, including without limitation responsibility for damages resulting from the use of or reliance on this work. Use of the information and instructions contained in this work is at your own risk. If any code samples or other technology this work contains or describes is subject to open source licenses or the intellectual property rights of others, it is your responsibility to ensure that your use thereof complies with such licenses and/or rights.

ISBN: 978-1-4919-0251-6

[TI]

This book is dedicated to my mother and father

*And if that one dream should fall and break into a thousand pieces,
never be afraid to pick up one of the pieces and begin again.
Each piece can be a new dream to believe in and to reach for. This is
life's way of touching you and giving you strength.*

—FLAVIA WEEDN

[*Contents*]

[*Foreword by Steve Souders*]

The next major milestone in the adoption of performance best practices is evangelism within the design community.

When I started collecting performance best practices, I focused on optimizations that did *not* impact the amount of content on the page. I wanted to avoid the "performance versus design" debate. (I knew the designers would win!) Within this constraint, there are still many optimizations that significantly improve performance: gzip, CDNs, caching headers, lossless image optimization, domain sharding, and more.

That was 2004. Today, many of those obvious optimizations are in place. And yet the size and complexity of websites grows at a rate that makes it a challenge to deliver a fast, pleasant user experience. Making today's websites fast requires considering the performance impact of richer, more dynamic, and more portable web content. Luckily, developers and designers share a drive to deliver the best user experience possible. This is the fertile ground that awaits you in Lara's book, *Designing for Performance*.

There's no question that a website's aesthetics are critical to delivering a compelling user experience. Now, after 10 years of gathering best practices, highlighting success stories, and evangelizing the need for speed, web performance is also recognized as being critical. It's time to discuss design and performance together—not as a debate, but as a collaboration that results in a beautiful user experience.

I use the word *beautiful* intentionally. The design of a website, its aesthetics, is often described with words like *beautiful, refreshing, compelling,* and *exciting*. Those descriptors are equally applicable to the experience of a fast website. After experiencing the *sluggishness* and *frustration* of a slower alternative, users find that an optimized website is also a beautiful experience.

Thanks to *Designing for Performance*, designers and developers have a framework for their collaboration. Lara outlines the questions that need to be answered, and the means for answering them. She provides numerous examples of the trade-off discussions that lay ahead and how successful teams have resolved them. Most important is that Lara compels us to start these discussions *early* in the design and development process, while code and mockups are still evolving and there's time to recognize and resolve performance challenges to deliver the beautiful experience that users deserve.

—Steve Souders, Fastly Chief Performance Officer
Author of *High Performance Websites* and *Even Faster Web Sites*

[*Foreword by Randy J. Hunt*]

Designers often lament when design is treated like "icing on a cake," a decorative layer to make something beautiful and desirable. Icing is applied at the end. Icing appears nonessential.

Inside is much more important, we think. The heart of the cake is where the flavor resides. The cake is named for what's under the icing (carrot), not the icing itself (cream cheese). Oh, the content! Soft, rich, flavorful content. We fall out of love with the icing. We, the designers, are focused on "more important things."

Time passes, and we come around. We argue with our younger selves. There *is* value in the icing. Oh, that icing! It tells people what to think and how to feel about the cake, even before they try it. It is the primary interface to the cake.

More time passes, and again we come around. The icing and the cake are meant to live in harmony. They complement each other. The icing holds the layers together. The layers give the icing a foundation, a purpose, and volume. We start worrying as much about the icing as the cake inside. Form and content, wed together in a satisfying whole.

And often, we stop there. Ta-da! We've done it—we've become an experienced, nuanced designer.

And yet we can't make a delicious cake. We haven't paid attention to the most important and most often overlooked details, the invisible ones. Are the ingredients of high quality? Are the ratios and timings right for the altitude, pan, and application? What ingredients do we combine when? What can we do to make the cake maintain its integrity while traveling?

Designed experiences are full of these seemingly invisible details. They're details we blissfully ignore, but we do so at the risk of not ever baking an excellent cake. They're the details that allow us to manipulate the context for the design itself. Sometimes they're deep in the technology (like the nuances of image compression), and sometimes they're outside the design (how a browser renders a web page).

The novice designer sees the surface. The experienced designer looks below the surface, at the content, the purpose. The enlightened designer understands the surface and the content, and pursues manipulation of the context.

Designing for Performance will help you understand and control the previously invisible attributes that make your design work well. It'll be delicious. Don't eat too fast, but please proceed with making your designs much, much faster.

—Randy J. Hunt, Creative Director, Etsy
Author of *Product Design for the Web*

[*Preface*]

If you are making decisions about the look and feel of a website, you are making decisions that directly impact the performance of that site, even if your job title doesn't include the word *designer*. Performance is a responsibility that can and should be shared across disciplines, as everyone at an organization impacts it. Whether it's convincing upper management that performance should be a priority, considering your options when weighing aesthetics and page speed in your day-to-day work, or educating and empowering other designers and developers within your organization, you have a large suite of tools and technology available to help you champion site speed.

Designers are in a unique position to impact overall page load time and perceived performance. The decisions that are made during the design process have an enormous impact on the end result of a site. I believe it's important for designers to understand the basics of page speed and the choices they have at their disposal to optimize their markup and images. I also believe it's imperative that designers weigh the balance between aesthetics and performance to improve the end user experience, and that everyone making changes to a site has the ability to measure the business metric impact of those changes.

After giving talks, workshops, and keynotes on frontend performance for years, I realized in talking with audience members that culture change is central to the performance topic. No one likes being a performance "cop" or "janitor"; these roles are unsuccessful in effecting long-lasting performance improvements on a site, since there are so many other people responsible for that site's user experience. While most of this book focuses on the technology and techniques behind making performance improvements, the final chapter is dedicated to performance as a cultural problem that cannot simply be solved with technology. Culture change is perhaps the hardest part of improving a site's performance.

Because I work at Etsy as an engineering manager, this book will include a number of references to Etsy and its engineering team's experiments. I currently manage the performance engineering team, and previously managed the mobile web engineering team. Throughout my career (and at Etsy) I've worked closely with many phenomenal designers, and I'm really excited to develop this resource specifically for them.

How This Book Is Organized

Within this book, we'll cover various online tools and software that can aid you as you make performance improvements. In chapters where image generation is covered, we'll use Photoshop within our examples rather than other kinds of image editing software.

In Chapter 1, we will cover the impact that page load time has on your site, your brand, and your audience's overall experience. Page load time is one of many factors that make up the user experience, and studies have shown that poor performance will negatively impact a site's engagement metrics. As more people are using mobile devices to access the Internet, a focus on performance will increase in priority, as mobile networks and hardware have a negative impact on page load time. Designers are in a unique position to improve page load time, and therefore, the overall user experience as well.

Chapter 2 covers the basics of page load time. It's important to have a foundation of knowledge regarding how browsers retrieve and render content for sites, as these are the main levers you can use to improve your site's performance. We'll also cover perceived performance, and how it differs from total page load time; the way users experience your site and perceive how quickly they can accomplish the one thing they want to do is an equally important metric to measure.

We'll walk through each of the main image formats used on the Web today within Chapter 3. We'll cover best practices for use and optimization for each file type. Included in this chapter are techniques to optimize the way images are loaded into web pages, such as spriting or replacing them with CSS or SVG. Lastly, we'll cover what you can do to increase the longevity of your optimized image solutions, including implementing style guides or automated workflows for image compression.

In Chapter 4, we will cover how to optimize the markup and styles implemented on your site. A thorough cleanup effort is incredibly important for both your HTML and CSS, followed by optimization of any web fonts used on your site. Focusing on creating clean, repurposable markup and documenting any design patterns will save both development time and page load time in the future as the site is edited or improved. We'll also cover the importance of load order, compression, and caching of your site's text assets.

Responsive web design is known for being "bad for performance," but it doesn't have to be! In Chapter 5, we'll walk through how important it is to be deliberate with the content, including images and fonts, you choose to load for your visitors across screen sizes. This chapter also covers how to approach responsive web design: create performance goals by breakpoint, use a mobile-first approach with your design, and measure your responsive design's performance at various screen sizes.

To understand the state of your site's user experience today as well as how it changes over time, it's imperative that you benchmark major performance metrics routinely. Chapter 6 will detail various browser plug-ins, synthetic testing, and real user monitoring tools and how they can help you measure your site's performance. Using these tools continuously as your site evolves to measure changes in performance and document why these changes occurred can help you and others learn about what impacts *your* site's performance.

In Chapter 7, we'll outline the various challenges you'll encounter when weighing aesthetics and performance. There are operational costs to consider, user behaviors to measure, and plenty of open-ended questions to ask when it comes to making these hard decisions. However, equipped with performance knowledge, a solid workflow, and experiments, you can make design and development decisions that result in an excellent overall user experience.

The largest hurdle to creating and maintaining stellar site performance is the culture of your organization. No matter the size or type of organization, it can be a challenge to educate, incentivize, and empower designers, developers, and management. We'll cover how you can shape the performance culture of your organization and create performance champions in Chapter 8.

Safari® Books Online

Safari Books Online (*http://safaribooksonline.com*) is an on-demand digital library that delivers expert content in both book and video form from the world's leading authors in technology and business. Technology professionals, software developers, web designers, and business and creative professionals use Safari Books Online as their primary resource for research, problem solving, learning, and certification training.

Safari Books Online offers a range of product mixes and pricing programs for organizations, government agencies, and individuals. Subscribers have access to thousands of books, training videos, and prepublication manuscripts in one fully searchable database from publishers like O'Reilly Media, Prentice Hall Professional, Addison-Wesley Professional, Microsoft Press, Sams, Que, Peachpit Press, Focal Press, Cisco Press, John Wiley & Sons, Syngress, Morgan Kaufmann, IBM Redbooks, Packt, Adobe Press, FT Press, Apress, Manning, New Riders, McGraw-Hill, Jones & Bartlett, Course Technology, and dozens more. For more information about Safari Books Online, please visit us *online*.

How to Contact Us

Please address comments and questions concerning this book to the publisher:

O'Reilly Media, Inc.
1005 Gravenstein Highway North
Sebastopol, CA 95472
800-998-9938 (in the United States or Canada)
707-829-0515 (international or local)
707-829-0104 (fax)

We have a web page for this book, where we list errata, examples, and any additional information. You can access this page at:

http://bit.ly/design-performance

To comment or ask technical questions about this book, send email to:

bookquestions@oreilly.com

For more information about our books, courses, conferences, and news, see our website at *http://www.oreilly.com*.

Find us on Facebook: *http://facebook.com/oreilly*

Follow us on Twitter: *http://twitter.com/oreillymedia*

Watch us on YouTube: *http://www.youtube.com/oreillymedia*

Acknowledgments

I want to thank everyone at Etsy for their support of this book, particularly my mobile web teammates (Jeremy, Amy, Chris, and Mike) and my performance teammates (Allison, Jonathan, Natalya, Dan, Seth, Daniel, and John). I also want to thank Courtney Nash; without her consideration and encouragement, this book wouldn't have seen the light of day.

Major thanks to the O'Reilly team: Mary Treseler, Angela Rufino, and Allyson MacDonald on the editing side, and Betsy Waliszewski, Sonia Zapien, Sophia DeMartini, and Audra Montenegro on the conference side. You all have made this process a blast.

The following reviewers were invaluable during the entire writing process: Jason Huff, Jonathan Klein, Brad Frost, Jason Grigsby, Christian Crumlish, Ilya Grigorik, Barbara Bermes, Guy Podjarny, Kim Bost, and Andy Davies. Thanks to Mat Marquis for his notes, patience, and knowledge of responsive images.

Thanks to Masha for her honesty, encouragement, and counsel. A special thanks goes out to my parents, who let me go and get a philosophy degree, which gave me the tools I needed to write a book. Their support throughout my career has been invaluable, and I feel incredibly proud to be their kid. Lastly, thanks to the 7th Avenue Donut Shop & Luncheonette, which made it possible for me to celebrate writing progress with their donuts.

[1]

Performance Is User Experience

Think about how you search for things on the Web. How quick are you to close a tab and go to the next search engine result if a site takes too long to load? If you're searching for local weather or news, how likely is it that you'll return to a site that waits forever to show relevant information on your screen? As you run errands and check your phone, how likely are you to have the patience to endure long load times as you try to check your email, compare prices, or search for directions? The less time you have, the higher your expectations are for a site to load quickly.

Page speed is increasingly important for websites. If you're looking for a page load time benchmark for your site, this is it: users expect pages to load in two seconds, and after three seconds, up to 40% of users will abandon your site (*http://bit.ly/1ttKspI*). Moreover, 85% of mobile users expect sites to load at least as fast or faster than sites on their desktop (*http://bit.ly/1ttKCO3*). As you design and build a website, or as you examine your existing site, how are you stacking up against these expectations?

Web performance *is* user experience. As you design and develop a new site, you'll consider many components of its user experience: layout, hierarchy, intuitiveness, ease of use, and more. Your site's experience determines how much your audience trusts your brand, returns to your site, and shares it with others. Page load time and how fast your site *feels* is a large part of this user experience and should be weighed equally with the aesthetics of your site.

Let's walk through some studies and data on how performance impacts end user experience.

Impact on Your Brand

The overall user experience affects your audience's impression of your brand. Akamai has reported that 75% of online shoppers who experience an issue such as a site freezing, crashing, taking too long to load, or having a convoluted checkout process will not buy from that site (*http://bit.ly/1ttKKNf*). Gomez studied online shopper behavior (*http://bit.ly/1ttKspI*) and found that 88% of online consumers are less likely to return to a site after a bad experience. The same study found that "at peak traffic times, more than 75% of online consumers left for a competitor's site rather than suffer delays." Are you losing users to your competitors' sites as you compete in page load time and other aspects of your site's user experience? Are you sure that your site is faster than your competitors'?

RETURNING USERS

Web performance impacts more than just ecommerce sites; improvements from page speed optimization apply to any kind of site. Users will return to faster sites, as evidenced in a study by Google (*http://bit.ly/1ttKPR8*) that noted a decrease in searches by users who experienced a site slowdown. Users who experienced a 400-millisecond delay performed 0.44% fewer searches during the first three weeks and 0.76% fewer searches during the second three weeks of the experiment.

Further, even when users who experienced the slowdown were removed from the experiment and saw the fast experience again, they took a while to return to their previous search usage level. The impact of page load time lasts even beyond the initial poor experience; users instinctively remember how it felt to browse that site and make choices about how often to return or use it afterward based on their experience.

SEARCH ENGINE RANKINGS

Additionally, page load time is factored into search engine results, bumping faster sites higher in the results list than slower sites. Google includes site speed in its search result ranking algorithm (*http://bit.ly/1ttKRsm*). Though Google makes it clear that it weighs content relevancy more heavily when ranking search results, page load time still contributes to the overall user experience of your site. Google wants to return results that are, overall, the best experience for its users.

Ignoring the page speed of your site is more than just a missed opportunity; it could be detrimental to users remembering your brand. Microsoft conducted a study (*http://bit.ly/1ttKUEA*) to see how users recall sites found in search results. A half hour after participants in the study entered a self-generated query into a search box, they received an emailed survey that asked them to recall the result list without referring back to it. The results of this survey showed that one of the two main factors affecting how likely a result was to be remembered was *where in the result list it was ranked*. Improving your page load time can improve your search engine result ranking, which is excellent for your brand.

Brand and digital product designer Naomi Atkinson brilliantly describes how design agencies can leverage performance in their pitch to a client, saying, "a large percentage of agencies are missing out on a key selling point. Pitching how quick they plan on making their client's website or service (and how), alongside their marketing and visual ideas, would make a world of difference. To their own success, and their clients." Performance is part of the overall user experience, and can have a huge impact on a company's brand.

Impact on Mobile Users

As more users move to mobile devices and more tasks move online, your site's overall user experience increases in importance. When we look at data from StatCounter Global Stats (*http://gs.statcounter.com/*), we can see that mobile is steadily increasing as a total percentage of Internet traffic (Figure 1-1).

Some companies are already seeing this substantial increase in traffic from mobile devices; according to Mary Meeker's Internet Trends report (*http://slidesha.re/1ttKWvZ*), 45% of transactions on Groupon came from mobile devices as of early 2013, which was up from less than 15% two years earlier. At Etsy, where I run the performance engineering team, 50% of user traffic comes from mobile devices as of early 2014.

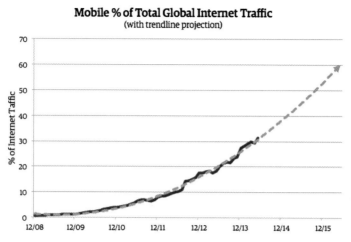

Figure 1-1. In this data from StatCounter Global Stats, we can see that the total percentage of Internet traffic coming from mobile devices is steadily increasing. As we extend a trendline forward, we can see that mobile usage growth probably won't be slowing anytime soon.

The percentage of mobile traffic is growing for nearly every site, and this will highlight page load time issues across the Internet, particularly for handset users. One study (*http://slidesha.re/eW8wQ9*) showed that handsets are the primary Internet access method for a vast number of global Internet users. Roughly 50% of Internet users in Africa and Asia are mobile-only, in contrast to 25% in the United States. This study classified "mobile-only" users as those who never or infrequently use the desktop Internet (the study included tablets in the "desktop" category). The bottom line: lots of people are primarily using handsets to access the Internet, and these devices present their own unique set of challenges.

MOBILE NETWORKS

The first reason why handsets take longer to load web pages is how mobile data is transmitted. Before a mobile device can transmit or receive data, it has to establish a radio channel with the network (see Figure 1-2). This can take *several seconds* over a 3G connection. After the device talks to a radio tower to negotiate when it can transmit data, the network carrier must transmit data from the tower to its internal network and then to the public Internet. The combination of these steps can easily add tens to thousands of milliseconds of extra latency. Further, if there is no data transmitted or received on the radio channel, a timeout causes the channel to become idle. This requires a new channel to be established and the entire process to restart, potentially wreaking havoc on web page load times.

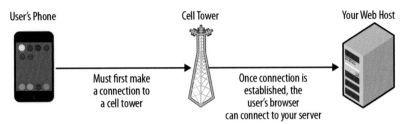

Figure 1-2. Before a mobile device can retrieve the assets needed to load a site, the device must establish a radio channel with the network. This process can take several seconds, and can wreak havoc on your page load times.

As Ilya Grigorik writes (*http://bit.ly/1ttL5je*), "when it comes to your web browsing experience, it turns out that latency, not bandwidth, is likely the constraining factor today." The more latency a user experiences, the longer it takes to make a round trip from the user's device to get data, and the longer it will take for a page to completely load. We'll walk through more about the basics of page speed in Chapter 2.

What Are Latency and Bandwidth?

Latency is the amount of time it takes for a packet of data to get from one point to another. For example, there is latency between the time it takes a host server to receive and process a request, and latency between the server sending an asset back and a browser receiving it. Latency is bound by fundamental physical properties (such as the speed of light). This delay is often measured in milliseconds (one millisecond is a thousandth of a second).

Bandwidth is the maximum throughput of a communication path, such as how much data can be transferred at once over fiber-optic cables or your mobile carrier. As an analogy, a taxi and a bus on a shared route have the same latency, but the bus has higher bandwidth.

While it's true that networks are slowly getting faster over time, your users on mobile devices may currently have a painful experience trying to get your site to load. On a typical United States desktop using WiFi, a request's average round trip takes just 50 milliseconds (*http://*

slidesha.re/1ttLhPw). This is the time it takes for a browser to send a request and the server to send a response over the network. However, on a mobile network, round-trip time can be more than 300 milliseconds. To get a feel for what this means: it's about as slow as old dial-up connections.

Add the round-trip time for each request it takes to load your site to the amount of time it takes to initially establish a radio channel with the network (potentially 1,000 to 2,000 milliseconds), and you can see how mobile network performance directly impacts your site's user experience. Further, it's hard to predict when wireless networks may be unreliable due to factors like a user being at a crowded event or in an area with poor reception.

This means you really need to prioritize performance as you optimize your site's design for mobile devices, as page load time has a significant impact on mobile users' experience and how they choose to use your site. This is evidenced by a number of companies' studies. My team at Etsy found an increased bounce rate of 12% on mobile devices when we added 160 KB of hidden images to a page. DoubleClick, a Google ad product, removed one client-side redirect (*http://bit.ly/1ttLjqx*) and saw a 12% increase in click-through rate on mobile devices. One of the great parts about focusing on performance benefits for mobile users is that these optimizations will also benefit your users who visit your site on any kind of device.

MOBILE USAGE PATTERNS

Your site's user experience will be impacted by page load time, regardless of the type of device used to access it. However, a negative user experience due to slow load times will be exacerbated if your user is on a mobile device, thanks to poorer network speeds as well as the different behaviors that mobile users exhibit.

A study by Google (*http://bit.ly/1ttLsdz*) found that people use smartphones in the following contexts:

- On-the-go as well as at home

- To communicate and connect

- In short bursts of time

- When they need information quickly and immediately

Tablets are similarly used for entertainment and browsing. Desktops, on the other hand, are used for more serious or research-intensive tasks. According to the study, smartphones are the most common starting place for the following online activities:

- Searching for specific information

- Browsing

- Shopping

- Social networking

As you design a site, consider how easily users will be able to complete tasks like these given the amount of time they plan to spend on their device in this sitting, and how significantly their mobile network may affect their ability to do so. Also remember that mobile-only users have no choice but to use their phone for all types of tasks, and that *all* users dislike having their time wasted, regardless of the device they are using. Your design should be intuitive and easy to use, and it should also become interactive as quickly as possible, no matter the platform.

MOBILE HARDWARE

Additionally, even when using WiFi on a handset, the user will likely have a slower experience due to antenna length and output power. WiFi can make use of more than one antenna at a time to send and receive signals; however, most smartphones aren't configured to take advantage of the multipath technology. Further, the WiFi antennas in laptops and desktops are significantly longer than those in handsets.

Handsets also attempt to be efficient with battery power (which is a big part of the smartphone user experience), and one way for them to conserve energy is by limiting the output of their radio. Desktops don't run on battery power, so they are able to use WiFi without making the same modifications to WiFi strength. Lastly, most smartphones currently in circulation support older and slower WiFi standards, rather than the most recent standard, 802.11ac, which only newer handsets support.

Many of the optimizations that improve page load time also improve device energy consumption, further improving the user experience. Things like WiFi signal strength, JavaScript rendering, and rendering of images all impact battery drain on mobile devices. In one study (*http://bit.ly/1ttLtOC*), researchers found that if Amazon converted all of its image files to JPEGs at 92% quality compression, it would save

20% of the energy needed to load its home page on an Android phone, and Facebook would save 30% doing the same. This change would positively impact the user experience by reducing energy consumption with no noticeable image quality loss. Another study (*http://bit. ly/1ttLxOt*) found that up to 35% of page load time in the critical path is spent on computation like HTML parsing and JavaScript execution on mobile devices.

The bottom line is that your efforts to optimize your site have an effect on the entire experience for your users, including battery life.

Designers' Impact on Performance

The length of the delay between when users enter a URL, click a button, or select from a drop-down list and when the web page responds will affect their perception of the site. A delay of less than 100 milliseconds feels instant to a user, but a delay between 100 and 300 milliseconds is perceptible. A delay between 300 and 1,000 milliseconds makes the user feel like a machine is working, but if the delay is above 1,000 milliseconds, your user will likely start to mentally context-switch.

These numbers matter because collectively we are designing sites with increasingly rich content: lots of dynamic elements, larger JavaScript files, beautiful animations, complex graphics, and more. You may focus on optimizing design and layout, but those can come at the expense of page speed. Some responsively designed sites are irresponsible with the amount of markup and images used to reformat a site for smaller screen sizes; they can unknowingly force their users to download unnecessary resources.

Designers who implement responsive web design are already making decisions about how content is displayed across screen sizes; these kinds of decisions significantly impact page load time, and responsive web design is a huge opportunity to insert performance considerations into the design workflow.

Think about your most recent design. How many different font weights were used? How many images did you use? How large were the image files, and what file formats did you use? How did your design affect the plan for markup and CSS structure?

The decisions made by designers are what typically drive the rest of how a website is built. The initial design phase includes decisions about:

- *Colors and gradients,* which impact image format choices, transparency needs, how many sprites can be created, and how much CSS3 is used

- *Layout,* which impacts the HTML hierarchy, class and ID names, the repurposability of design patterns, and the organization of CSS

- *Typography,* which impacts the weight and number of included font files

- *Design patterns,* which impact what can be repurposed and cached across the site, how and when assets are loaded, and ease of editability by future designers or developers

These kinds of decisions are often determined in the beginning of the product workflow, which is why they have a large impact on the final page load time. To illustrate this, let's say we have an example logo that we are planning to overlay on a div with a light blue background, as shown in Figure 1-3.

Figure 1-3. This example logo has a transparent background, and will be overlaid on a div with a light blue background.

The transparency and overlay requirements impact the file type and file size of this image. A designer who is considering page load time during the design stage can ask questions like, "What if I export it as a JPEG or PNG-8 with no transparency? What if I use a light blue matte on a PNG-8 file? How might that impact performance?" We can test exporting JPEG and PNG-8 versions and see the resulting file size for each in Figures 1-4 through 1-7.

Designing *for* Performance

Figure 1-4. Original PNG-24 with transparency: 7.6 KB.

Designing *for* Performance

Figure 1-5. PNG-8 with solid background: 5.0 KB.

Designing *for* Performance

Figure 1-6. PNG-8 with matte: 2.7 KB.

Designing *for* Performance

Figure 1-7. JPEG at 75% quality with solid background: 20.2 KB.

In these tests we can see that the different file formats result in different sizes due to their solid backgrounds or transparency. We will cover more about image optimizations and weighing your options in Chapter 3.

We have a huge opportunity to play around with potential performance wins and measure the impact of different design choices. In Chapter 3, we will cover how you can choose and compress a variety of image formats, and in Chapter 6 we'll walk through how to measure and iterate on designs with page load time in mind.

The performance of both new designs and redesigns are impacted by these kinds of decisions. Every existing site can be cleaned up and tested with performance in mind. On one site, I was able to cut page load time in half by cleaning CSS and optimizing images, normalizing site colors, and carefully reorganizing assets in an existing site template. Rather than redesigning the site, I simply focused on killing bloated HTML and CSS, which resulted in smaller HTML, CSS, and stylesheet image file sizes.

You can read more about how to clean HTML and CSS with an eye on performance in Chapter 4.

Even if your job title doesn't include the word *designer*, if you are making decisions about the look and feel of a website, you are making decisions that directly impact the performance of that site. Performance is a shared responsibility, and everyone on your team impacts it. Considering performance when making design decisions will have an enormous impact on your users. Weighing aesthetics and performance should be paramount in your design workflow, which we will cover in Chapter 7. This is also a huge opportunity for various disciplines within an organization to collaborate; designers and developers can work together to create a phenomenal user experience.

In the next chapter, we will walk through the basics of page load time, including how browsers fetch and render content. Understanding how your users' browsers communicate with your hosted files, how the file size of your site's files affect page load time, and how users perceive the performance of your site will significantly help you as you design a site and strive to find a balance between aesthetics and performance.

[2]

The Basics of Page Speed

As you design a site, it's important to know the basics of page speed so you can better understand what to optimize. Browsers fetch and display content in a fairly dependable manner; understanding how web pages are rendered will help you reliably predict how your design choices will impact your site's page speed. We'll aim to optimize for:

- The number of resources (like images, fonts, HTML, and CSS) loaded on a page
- The file size of these resources
- The perceived performance of your site by your users

In addition to what users see as their browser renders content, there are further improvements that you can make on the backend, including optimizing any work that the server needs to do to get the first byte back to the client. There's more that goes into page load time than just what happens on the frontend of your site, such as making calls to a database or compiling templates into HTML. However, as Steve Souders says, "80 to 90% of the end user response time is spent on the frontend." As this is where the vast majority of the user experience lives, we'll be focusing on the frontend aspects of page load time.

How Browsers Render Content

Between the moment your users enter your site's URL into their browser and the moment the page starts to reveal your site design, their browser and your web host negotiate all the data that they need to communicate to each other.

First, the browser sends out a request to get some content. The first time the browser makes a request to a new domain, it needs to find the server where this content lives. This is called a *DNS lookup*. The DNS lookup figures out where on the Internet your web host lives so that the request for content can make it all the way to your server. A browser will remember this location for a set period of time (determined by the DNS settings for your server) so that it doesn't need to spend valuable time doing this lookup for every request.

Once your server makes a connection to the user's browser and receives its first request, it'll decode the request and locate the content that the browser is looking for as it tries to render the page. Your server will then send back this content, whether it be an image, CSS, HTML, or another kind of asset, and the browser will begin downloading it and rendering the page for the user. Figure 2-1 illustrates this cycle.

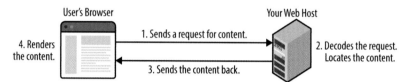

Figure 2-1. A page load time cycle between your user's browser and the content on your server.

The first byte of content that the browser receives is measured and called *time to first byte* (TTFB). It's a good indicator of how quickly the backend of your site is able to process and send back content. On the frontend, once your browser begins to receive that content back from your server, it can still take some time to download and render the content on the page. Some file types are quick for browsers to process and render; other kinds of requests (like blocking JavaScript) may need to be fully processed before a user's browser can continue to render additional content.

These content requests can vary in size and order. Browsers are smart and try to parallelize requests for content to the server in order to reduce the time it takes to render your web page. However, there are a lot of things we can do to optimize this process of requesting and retrieving your site's content so that your site becomes interactive as quickly as possible for your users.

REQUESTS

Optimizing the size and number of requests that it takes to create your web page will make a tremendous impact on your site's page load time. To illustrate how requests affect total page speed, let's look at an example waterfall chart using WebPagetest (*http://www.WebPagetest. org/*). (We will walk through how to use WebPagetest in Chapter 6.) A waterfall chart such as Figure 2-2 shows you how much time it takes to request the contents of a page, such as CSS, images, or HTML, and how much time it takes to download this content before displaying it in a browser.

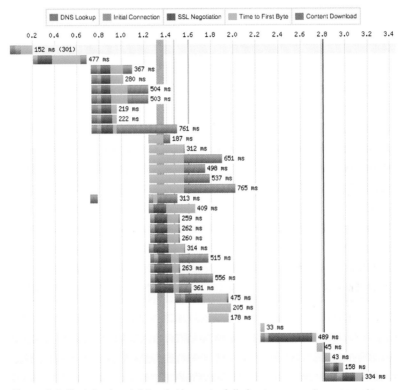

Figure 2-2. Each horizontal line in the waterfall chart represents a separate asset request.

Each horizontal line in the waterfall chart represents a separate asset request, such as the HTML, a stylesheet, a script, or an image. Our first request, usually for the HTML of a page, will include a DNS lookup, as the browser needs to figure out where on the Web this content lives. Each subsequent request will then have an initial connection time to the server where the file is hosted, then some time before the first byte back is received by the user's browser, and then additional time to download and display the content.

Naturally, the larger the piece of requested content is, the longer it will take to download, be processed by the browser, and be displayed on a page. Also, the more independent pieces of content are needed to render the page, the more time it will take for the page to fully load. This is why we will aim to optimize both the size and number of image, CSS, and JavaScript files that are required for your site to load.

For example, when we work with images, we can organize separate image requests into a single *sprite* (i.e., collection of images) to cut down on the number of requests that the browser needs to make (we'll cover this technique in "Sprites"). We can also run every image through compression tools that reduce the images' file size without compromising their quality (read more in "Additional Compression"). We'll also focus on reducing the total number of CSS and JavaScript files, and loading them in the best order possible for perceived performance, as described in "CSS and JavaScript Loading." Optimizing the size and number of requests that your browser needs to load your page will help you optimize your site's speed.

CONNECTIONS

The number of *requests* that it takes to load your page is different than the number of *connections* your browser makes to retrieve this content. In WebPagetest, the Connection view (Figure 2-3) shows each connection to a server and the requests that are retrieved over it.

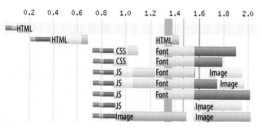

Figure 2-3. The Connection view in WebPagetest shows each connection to a server and the requests that are retrieved.

For each connection, you may see a DNS lookup for the domain (dark green), an initial connection to the server (orange), and possibly an SSL negotiation before the browser begins to retrieve the content (hot pink) for assets served over HTTPS. But browsers are smart and try to optimize downloads of content once they have that connection open to your server.

What Is an SSL Negotiation?

An *SSL negotiation* happens when a browser makes a secure request for content, also known as an *encrypted HTTPS connection*. The user's browser and server negotiate encrypted keys and certificates to establish a secure connection between each other. Because this SSL negotiation requires exchanges between the browser and your server, it adds page load time.

You'll notice that in each row, there are multiple kinds of files being downloaded. This is known as a *persistent connection*, as the browser is able to keep a connection open and reuse it for another request. Your browser fetches some JavaScript, then uses this open connection to also grab a font file, and then an image, before needing to establish another new connection to get more content.

You'll also notice that the browser (Chrome, in this case) has established multiple open connections at the same time, parallelizing the amount of content it can fetch. The number of simultaneous persistent connections each browser can make varies. Modern browsers allow up to six simultaneous open connections (Chrome, Firefox, Opera 12) or eight (Internet Explorer 10).

It's important to see how many connections it takes to load your page. If you see lots of connections, then your content may be spread out over too many domains, which prevents your browser from optimizing open connections. Calling lots of third-party scripts is one way this can happen.

Use waterfall charts to assess how well your page is loading in combination with measuring your total page weight and the perceived performance of your page. Read more about WebPagetest's waterfalls and how to find buggy content loading in Chapter 6.

Page Weight

The file size of HTML, images, and other content needed to load your page will have an effect on the total page load time. One way to measure the file size of each kind of content is to use the browser plug-in YSlow. We'll walk through how to use it in "YSlow."

After you run YSlow on your page, switch to the Components tab (Figure 2-4) to see a list of the content types for this page and how large they are.

↑ TYPE	SIZE (KB)	GZIP (KB)
⊟ doc (1)	3.4K	
doc	3.4K	1.5K
⊟ js (1)	40.1K	
js	40.1K	15.8K
⊟ css (1)	4.8K	
css	4.8K	1.5K
⊞ cssimage (1)	11.5K	
⊞ image (6)	722.6K	
⊞ favicon (1)	2.0K	

Figure 2-4. In the Components tab within YSlow, you can see a list of the content types used on a web page and how large they are.

In this example, we can see that having gzip turned on decreases the size of our HTML ("doc" in this table), JavaScript, and CSS files. If you're curious about how gzip works, we'll cover that in "Minification and gzip." We can also see that though there are only six images needed to load the page, they total 722.6 KB! Those are some very large images. The "cssimage" row separates any images called and applied via CSS from the images embedded directly in the site's HTML.

Take a look at your own page weight, and compare it to the "average bytes per page" graphs at *http://httparchive.org/interesting.php*. Are you using a lot of CSS or JavaScript? What's the breakdown of content types on your page—do your images vastly outweigh the other content types as in the preceding example, or is there another outlier?

What Is the HTTP Archive?

The *HTTP Archive* is a permanent repository of web performance information such as size of pages, failed requests, and technologies utilized. It gathers WebPagetest information for URLs included in the Alexa Top 250,000 sites.

There are no hard-and-fast rules about page weight; however, it's important to keep track of your page weight over time to make sure that there are no large and surprising changes as your site evolves and more content is added or the design iterates. We'll talk through lots more about measuring and iterating on your site's page weight and load time in "Changes over Time."

Look at the total page weight and the breakdown of different kinds of content in combination with the number of requests it takes to load your page and the perceived performance of your page. The amount of content needed to render your page will directly impact how long it takes to load for your users—the smaller, the better.

Perceived Performance

The perception of how fast your website loads is more important than how long it *actually* takes to load. Users' perception of speed will be based on how quickly they start to see content render on the page, how quickly it becomes interactive, and how smoothly the site scrolls.

CRITICAL RENDERING PATH

When your user initially loads a page, it will be blank. Blank space is a poor user experience; it makes the user feel like nothing is happening. To fix this user experience issue, you'll need to optimize your *critical rendering path*.

To understand how the critical rendering path works, you need to understand how browsers craft the visual rendering of web pages by reading the HTML, CSS, and JavaScript for a page. Browsers start by creating the *Document Object Model*, or DOM. A browser will receive the HTML back from a web server and begin parsing it: raw bytes become characters, strings of characters become tokens like <body>, tokens become objects that have properties and rules, and finally these objects are linked together into a data structure. This last step is the creation of the DOM tree, which a user's browser relies on for all further processing of the page.

As the browser reads through the HTML, it'll bump into a stylesheet. The browser will pause everything and go request this file from your server. When it receives the file back, the browser will repeat a similar process: raw bytes become characters, strings of characters become tokens, tokens become objects, objects are linked in a tree structure, and we'll finally have a *CSS Object Model*, or CSSOM.

Next, the user's browser will combine the DOM and the CSSOM to create a *render tree*, which it'll use to compute the size and position of every visible element. The render tree contains only what is necessary to render the page (so anything with display: none will not be included in the render tree). Lastly, the browser will display the final render tree on the screen.

This entire process captures the critical rendering path that browsers work through to display content to a user. One way to see how long it takes for a user to begin to see your site load is the "Start Render" metric in WebPagetest, which tells you how many seconds it took for the browser to begin rendering content.

With WebPagetest, we can look at the filmstrip view of a page (Figure 2-5) and see what is visible over time as it loads.

Figure 2-5. With WebPagetest's filmstrip view, you can see what is visible on the user's screen as a page loads over time.

As we look at the Yahoo! home page in 0.5-second intervals, we can see that the page is blank until roughly 2 seconds into loading time. The sooner you can begin to get visible content on the page, the quicker the page will feel to your user.

[NOTE]

WebPagetest results will vary by location, browser, connection speed, and other factors. While it's easy to look at the loading of the Yahoo! home page over 0.5-second intervals, you'll likely want to look at 0.1-second intervals of your own site's load time, which you can choose from WebPagetest's filmstrip view.

There are a few ways to optimize your critical rendering path. Since, by default, CSS is treated as a render-blocking resource, use media types and media queries to indicate which parts of your CSS can be non-render-blocking:

```
<link href="main.css" rel="stylesheet">
<link href="print.css" rel="stylesheet" media="print"> ❶
<link href="big-screens.css" rel="stylesheet"
  media="(min-width: 61.5em)"> ❷
```

1. This stylesheet will apply only when the page is being printed. It will not block rendering when the page is first loaded.

2. This stylesheet will apply only when the browser's width is equal to or greater than 61.5 em. It will not block rendering when the width of the browser is less than 61.5 em, but it will block rendering if the browser meets this min-width condition.

Another way to optimize your critical rendering path is to ensure that you are loading JavaScript in the most efficient way possible. JavaScript blocks DOM construction unless it is declared as asynchronous; read more about how to make your JavaScript play nicely with the rest of page load in "CSS and JavaScript Loading."

Want more insight into the perceived performance impact of the critical path on your site? WebPagetest will also give you a metric called "Speed Index" (*http://bit.ly/1ttMTJ5*) for your page. According to WebPagetest's documentation, Speed Index is the average time at which visible parts of the page are displayed. It's expressed in milliseconds and is dependent on the size of the chosen viewport.

The Speed Index metric is an excellent one to watch as you try to measure the perceived performance of your page, as it will tell you how quickly the "above the fold" content is populated for your users. It's good to focus on how quickly your users begin to see and be able to interact with content rather than focus how long it takes for the browser to completely finish loading your page's content (which includes any asynchronous content that is fetched and executed after the document is visually complete). You can read more about WebPagetest's measuring of Speed Index and how long it takes to fully load a page in Chapter 6.

Time to interactivity is a term for the time between when users navigate to a page and when they can complete an action like clicking a link, performing a search, or playing a video. There are a number of ways you can improve the speed at which content begins to load and become interactive for your users by optimizing the critical rendering path:

- Asynchronously load content
- Prioritize requests for "above the fold" content
- Follow best practices for loading CSS and JavaScript (more in "CSS and JavaScript Loading")
- Cache assets for returning users (more in "Caching Assets")
- Ensure that any primary actions for the page are available to the user as quickly as possible

By optimizing the critical rendering path in concert with the other aspects of total page load time, you can ensure that your user has a positive impression of how quickly your site loads.

JANK

Have you ever noticed stuttering or skipping as you're scrolling down a web page? This is referred to as *jank*, and it occurs when browser rendering slows down below 60 frames per second. Jank will create a poor user experience and will negatively affect your users' perception of your site performance.

This stuttering is due to the browser's attempt to paint a change on the page. Changing visual properties of an element (such as its background, color, border radius, or shadow) will trigger a new paint in the browser. Your user can also trigger paints by performing an action that changes the visibility of an element of your page, like showing or hiding content or clicking through a carousel. A browser will "repaint" parts of your user's screen as things change.

Sometimes, these repaints drastically affect your browser rendering, slowing it down below the 60-frames-per-second threshold. For example, some animations (such as position, scale, rotation, and opacity) can be handled by modern browsers within 60 frames per second; other animations may create jank for your user. Repaints are expensive operations for browsers, and will make your page feel sluggish.

If you notice that your site is showing symptoms of jank, there are some browser tools available to help you debug the root cause. There is a Timeline view in Chrome DevTools (Figure 2-6) that shows you the frame rate as you interact with a page.

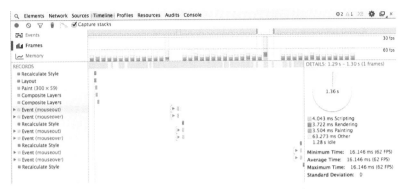

Figure 2-6. Chrome DevTools' Timeline view shows you the frame rate over time as you interact with a web page.

Once you click "record" and begin interacting with your page, Chrome DevTools will record the frames per second as well as what the browser was doing, such as recalculating styles, firing events, or painting. Once you find an area where the frame rate decreased below the 60-frames-per-second threshold, you can begin targeting that area to reduce repaint issues. Start by hiding elements on this area of the page to see which elements may be triggering the jank, and then play with hiding colors, shadows, and animations to see what may be the root cause of the sluggishness. Read more about how to use Chrome DevTools in "Chrome DevTools."

When it comes to users' perception of your site's performance, make sure that you and others are routinely testing pages from various locations and devices. Are you able to accomplish a page's primary task quickly, or are you finding that your site *feels* slow? Are you noticing sluggishness in a certain browser or mobile device? Conducting some user testing can also help you figure out which parts of your page should load the quickest, and which need further optimization to improve the perceived performance and critical rendering path.

If you find that users perceive your site as slow to load because they're spending a long time staring at a blank page, or becoming impatient while waiting for an area to become clickable, you can focus on optimizing the load order and size of page requests. If the page becomes interactive more quickly and starts to show content faster above the fold, the perceived performance of your site improves, creating a better user experience.

Other Impacts on Page Speed

In addition to performance factors that are in your control, there are a number of environmental factors that also impact your site's page load time, including a user's geographic location, network, and browser.

GEOGRAPHY

A user's geographic location may greatly impact the amount of time it takes to load your site. If you run multiple tests on various geographic locations using a testing tool like WebPagetest, you'll notice a spectrum of load times. This is due to the fact that browsers are requesting and receiving data via physical connections, and there is a limit to the speed at which content can travel over long distances; it will take longer for your user's browser to contact your server if it's farther away. If a user is in Australia and your content lives on a server in the United States, it will take much longer for that user to access your content than it would for someone living in the United States.

This is why *content delivery networks* (CDNs) are used by sites that have a global user base. CDNs set up servers with copies of data around the world so that users can contact the server that is closest to them, saving time. For the Australian user base in this example, you can consider serving your content from a CDN with a location in the Asia/ Pacific region so that users can access your content from a server closer to where they live.

NETWORK

Depending upon where your users live, there may also be limitations to their bandwidth, or a cap on how much bandwidth they can consume in a given time period. The Internet infrastructure where they live might not be as stable or fast as the infrastructure that you use to test your site's speed. Remember that as you are testing your own site, it may not be a representative user experience for your actual user base, as you may have a significantly better Internet infrastructure, a faster connection speed, and a more powerful device.

Similarly, a user's network can have an enormous impact on how long it takes to make each request for content. On a slow network, it will take a much longer time for your user's browser to find and then make the initial connection to your server, and then even more time to download your content. This will multiply as the number of requests your user's browser must make to render your page increases. Mobile networks are a good example of the impact of network latency; read more about these challenges in "Mobile Networks."

BROWSER

Your user's browser may also impact the perceived performance of your site, as each browser handles requests and rendering of content slightly differently. Browsers that do not support progressive JPEGs (which we will cover in "JPEG") will wait until a progressive JPEG file is fully downloaded before showing it on the page, which feels much slower to users than showing a baseline JPEG. Browsers that support fewer parallel connections will request and render content more slowly than newer browsers that support significantly more connections at a time.

All of these environmental factors are out of your control. However, being deliberate about optimizing your site for the quickest load time possible and routinely testing your site's performance from various locations and devices will help you create the best user experience possible for your audience.

In the next chapter, we'll cover the biggest chunk of most sites' page weight: images. It's important to keep image formatting and compression in mind, especially now that you understand how page weight and requests affect your site's total page load time. The more you can optimize every image's size and how it's rendered by your user's browser, the better your site's user experience will be.

[3]

Optimizing Images

Images make up the majority of most sites' total page weight. The number of image bytes has grown by more than 30% on the average web page in the last year (*http://bit.ly/1ttROtq*), with very little growth in requests. Thanks to their relatively large file size and the number of images included on the average site (see Figure 3-1), optimizing images is arguably the easiest big win when it comes to improving your site's page load time.

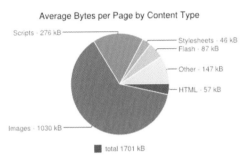

Figure 3-1. The HTTPArchive.org (*http://httparchive.org/interesting.php*) survey of page weight shows that images make up the majority of most sites' total page weight.

You can make substantial improvements to both your main content images as well as the images that make up your site design by:

- Finding the right balance of file size and quality for each image
- Looking for ways to reduce the total number of image requests on your site
- Optimizing your site's image creation workflows for performance improvements

Let's start by looking at the various image file types available, and then we'll examine the options you have for optimizing your site's images for page speed.

Choosing an Image Format

You have a range of file types to choose from when creating images for your site. When generating an image, ask yourself:

- How compressed can this image be without a noticeable quality reduction?

- How many colors are needed?

- Can I simplify this image in any way?

- Do I need any transparency?

- Do I need any animation?

- At what maximum height and width will this image be displayed?

- How will this image be repurposed across the site?

The most common image file formats on the Web are JPEG, GIF, and PNG. Table 3-1 outlines each popular image file format, how it's best used, and some optimization tips for it.

TABLE 3-1. Image format overview

FORMAT	BEST FOR	OPTIMIZATION OPTIONS
JPEG	Photos, images with many colors	Decrease quality, export as progressive, reduce noise
GIF	Animations	Decrease dithering, decrease number of colors, increase horizontal patterns, reduce vertical noise
PNG-8	Images with few colors	Decrease dithering, decrease number of colors, increase horizontal and vertical patterns
PNG-24	Partial transparency	Reduce noise, reduce number of colors

Let's walk through the pros and cons of each of these file formats as well as how to export and optimize each kind of image.

JPEG

JPEGs are the ideal file format for photographs or other images with a large spectrum of colors. JPEGs are designed to compress files in ways that our eyes won't notice at a high enough quality. At low quality, we'll notice artifacting, banding, and graininess in JPEG images, as JPEG is a *lossy* file format. Lossy file types discard pieces of information as they are saved; JPEGs choose which pieces of information to discard by using an algorithm based loosely on how humans see and perceive information.

What Is "Artifacting"?

An *artifact* is a loss of clarity within an area of an image. Artifacting may cause an image to look fuzzy, pixelated, or blurry.

JPEGs are very smart at discarding information over smooth gradients and areas of low contrast. Images with sharp contrasts between adjacent pixels are usually better suited for a different file format (such as PNG), since in a JPEG format you will likely see artifacting. But because JPEGs are excellent at creating relatively smaller files with a lot of information in them, it's no surprise that the majority of the images on the Web are JPEGs. The smart compression in JPEGs will generally result in a smaller file size for complex images, which is one of our goals as we work to improve how long it takes to load a web page.

With any image file you generate, test out a few different qualities and file types in the Save for Web workflow within Photoshop. You're aiming for a happy medium of acceptable quality and small file size. It's important to play with the file size and see what level of compression is noticeable. Look for artifacts, messy contrast between elements, and blurry details and text.

In Figure 3-2, we can see a zoomed-in portion of a photograph that has been exported at various qualities using Photoshop's Save for Web tool. As you compare the images exported at quality 25, 50, 75, and 100, notice that the lower qualities have more artifacting around the edges of high contrast.

Figure 3-2. In this comparison of Photoshop's Save for Web export quality, the lower-quality JPEG images have more artifacting around edges of high contrast, such as the green background surrounding the top white leaves.

Why Use "Save for Web"?

In Photoshop, you have two main ways to generate an image: the Save for Web tool, and Save As. Unlike Save As, Save for Web will provide additional optimizations for generated image files, and will also allow you to tweak the quality of the image and preview the result before saving. Save for Web will help you find a balance between aesthetics and file size for your images.

The more distinct colors in an image, the larger a JPEG's file size will be, as it is harder for the JPEG's algorithm to find easy areas in which to compress and blend colors. Noise and grain in a JPEG can greatly increase its file size, as you can see in Figure 3-3. When creating new images (particularly if you are creating repeating patterns), be judicious with the number of colors you are introducing.

Noise Amount: 5%
JPEG quality: 50%
File size: 1.56 KB

Noise Amount: 5%
JPEG quality: 75%
File size: 4.83 KB

Noise Amount: 10%
JPEG quality: 50%
File size: 2.98 KB

Noise Amount: 10%
JPEG quality: 75%
File size: 9.02 KB

Figure 3-3. Comparison of JPEG image noise, quality, and resulting file size.

In Figure 3-3, you can see a comparison of JPEGs that have been exported via Photoshop's Save for Web tool and then passed through ImageOptim, an additional image compression tool. Read more about compression tools in "Additional Compression." The original JPEG was a blue square with a Noise filter added within Photoshop. The left two images have an added noise amount of 5%, and the right two images have added noise at 10%.

Comparing the images, you can see that the exported JPEGs with less noise are also smaller in file size; the images with 10% noise are nearly double the file size of the images with 5% noise. Again, JPEG quality also has an effect on total file size. As you optimize for page load time, keep both noise and JPEG quality in mind, and see where you can find savings in your images.

Your choice of JPEG type can also affect the perceived performance of how fast your site loads (read more in "Perceived Performance"). *Baseline JPEGs* (those typically found on the Web) are a full-resolution, top-to-bottom scan of an image. *Progressive JPEGs* are made up of a series of scans of increasing quality.

Because baseline JPEGs are a top-to-bottom scan, they appear this way in the browser, with pieces of them being slowly revealed in rows. Progressive JPEGs, on the other hand, appear all at once at low quality; then this low-quality version of the image is replaced with versions of progressively higher quality. Progressive JPEGs appear to load faster than baseline JPEGs because they fill in the space necessary all at once with a low-quality version instead of loading the image in chunks.

Progressive JPEGs are displayed in all browsers. However, not all browsers render progressive JPEGs as quickly as we'd hope. In browsers that don't support progressive rendering, progressive JPEGs will display more slowly, as they appear after the file has completed downloading rather than progressively. In these cases, they will visually appear more slowly than baseline JPEGs, which arrive in stages. You can read more about progressive JPEG browser support in the PerfPlanet article "Progressive JPEGs: a new best practice" (*http://bit.ly/1ttThzL*).

One additional consideration when you are choosing a JPEG type is CPU usage. *Each* progressive scan requires about the same CPU power as one entire baseline JPEG would need to render on a page. On mobile devices, this can be a concern. Currently Mobile Safari does not render progressive JPEGs in a progressive manner, which is understandable considering the tax on the CPU. However, other mobile browsers, such as Chrome on Android, do render them progressively. Overall, progressive JPEGs are still an excellent improvement for the overall user experience, and the small CPU downside will likely be improved by browser vendors in the future.

If you're interested in testing existing images by converting baseline JPEGs to progressive JPEGs, there are tools like SmushIt (*http://www.smushit.com/*) that can help. To create a progressive JPEG from scratch using the Save for Web dialog in Photoshop, simply check the Progressive checkbox in the top-right area of the Save for Web window, near the Quality picker (see Figure 3-4).

Figure 3-4. Create a progressive JPEG by checking the Progressive checkbox in Photoshop's Save for Web window.

Lastly, be sure to run any exported JPEG through a compression tool after your initial export from Photoshop. You can gain additional file size savings at little or no quality loss. See "Additional Compression" for suggested compression tools and workflows.

GIF

GIFs are one of the oldest graphic file formats on the Web. The GIF file type was originally created in 1987 to store multiple bitmap images into a single file. It's since seen a resurgence in popularity, thanks to its ability to include animation. GIFs support transparency as well as animation, but include only up to 256 colors within a frame. If a GIF includes an animation, each frame can support a separate palette of up to 256 colors. Unlike JPEGs, GIFs are a *lossless* file format.

There are two rare circumstances when you may want to choose a GIF for your image file format:

- When the file size of the generated GIF is smaller than the file size of the same image generated as a PNG-8

- When an animation cannot be replaced with CSS3

When you create a GIF, you have a few options to play with as you try to find the balance between aesthetics and file size. First, you can choose a *dither* amount as well as the number of colors included in the palette within the Save for Web tool, as you can see in Figure 3-5.

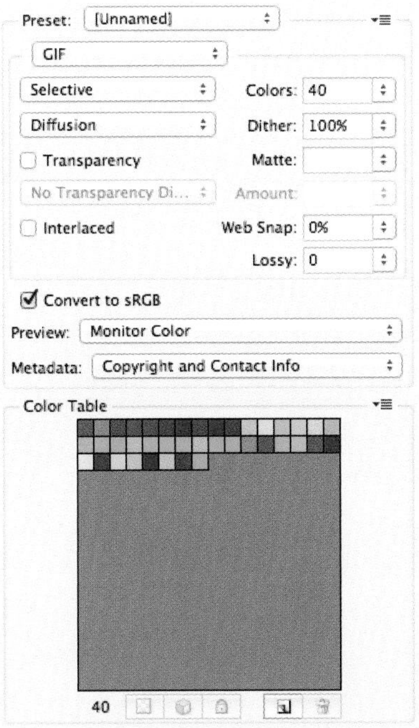

Figure 3-5. Creating a GIF in Photoshop.

Dithering helps create visually smoother transitions between colors. It examines adjacent pixels of different colors and chooses a new color somewhere in between to give the appearance of a smoother blend. For example, in this image with a maximum of 40 colors, you can see the smoothness with dithering set to 0 (Figure 3-6) versus the appearance with the dithering set to 100 (Figure 3-7).

Figure 3-6. GIF with dithering set to 0: 4.8 KB.

Figure 3-7. GIF with dithering set to 100: 9.7 KB.

The file size of the GIF is affected by the amount of dithering. In Figures 3-6 and 3-7, when dithering is set to 0, the exported GIF is 4.8 KB. When dithering is set to 100, the exported GIF is 9.7 KB. Note that though both had a maximum of 40 colors included in the Save for Web palette, you may have up to 256 colors within your palette.

Interestingly, if we change the direction of this colorful gradient in the GIF and export it with dithering set to 100, we see a large change in file size in Figure 3-8.

Figure 3-8. GIF with vertical patterns: 21 KB.

Why does the file size more than double in this case? GIFs follow a compression algorithm that removes horizontal redundancy. So by introducing extra vertical details or noise, we've increased the file size of the GIF. When you create a GIF, consider how successful it may be at optimizing your image and creating the smallest file size possible while still being aesthetically pleasing. Reduce vertical noise, as it will have a substantial impact on your GIF's file size.

For most images that contain few colors and sharp edges, PNG-8 will be your file format of choice. PNGs use a different kind of compression method than GIFs; they look for repeated horizontal patterns in the image like GIFs do, but in addition, they also look for vertical patterns. It's highly likely that a PNG-8 version of your image will be smaller in file size than a GIF, so be sure to test PNG-8 as you find a balance between file size and aesthetics.

Lastly, if you have a simple animation in a GIF, such as a spinner or loading indicator, consider replacing it with a CSS3 animation. CSS3 animations tend to be lighter weight and better for performance than GIFs, so it's worth testing to see if you can replace GIFs on your site.

PNG

PNG is a lossless image format designed to improve upon the GIF file format. Photoshop allows you to export PNG-8 and PNG-24 images; each format has pros and cons you need to consider when optimizing for performance.

When you need transparency in your image, PNG will be your best choice. GIFs also support transparency, but they tend to be much heavier than PNGs. PNGs recognize horizontal patterns and compress them like GIFs do, but they also can find vertical patterns, which means you can benefit from additional compression in PNGs.

When you have a small number of colors in your image, PNG-8 is likely going to be your best choice for file format. PNG-8 files contain a maximum of 256 colors within the image, and generally result in a smaller file size.

In Figure 3-9, you can see that the image contains 247 total colors. In this particular example, all 247 colors in our palette are various shades of gray. PNG-8 images can contain a maximum of 256 colors, like GIFs. Just as with a GIF, we can also select our dither amount (read more in "GIF"), which will affect the total file size.

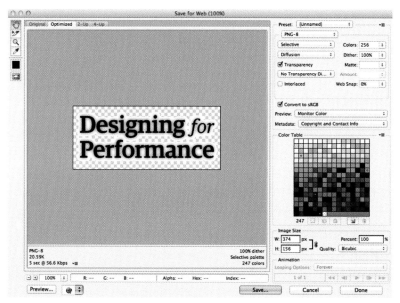

Figure 3-9. PNG-8 Export view in Photoshop.

We are also working with transparency in Figure 3-9. The text has a drop shadow, and the PNG-8 Export view has a white matte selected. The matte tells Photoshop what the background color of the image should be; this color should match the background of the element where you'll be placing the exported PNG. Photoshop is choosing which pixels need to be transparent and how the original translucent drop shadow blends with our chosen matte in order to color the other pixels surrounding the text.

In Figure 3-10, we set the PNG to contain a maximum of 256 colors, but again we don't need all 256. In this case, the PNG will export with just 4: white, blue, green, and red. Even though we've selected Transparency, the image actually doesn't need it, as it has a white background exported as part of the image. Photoshop works to help you create an optimized file size of your image, but you'll still need to run it through additional compression tools (read more in "Additional Compression").

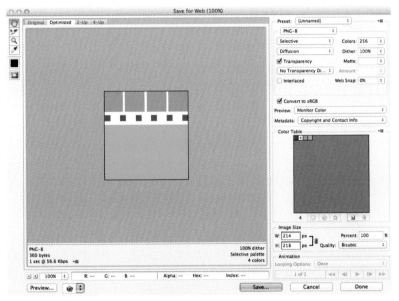

Figure 3-10. PNG-8 Export view with few colors.

PNG-24 files, on the other hand, do not have the same restriction in color palette. While you can use PNGs for photos, they will often be 5 to 10 times larger in file size than JPEGs because they are lossless. Just as with any other kind of image file, reducing noise and the number of colors will be beneficial to the overall file size of your PNGs. Let's compare the two images in Figure 3-11: one with 5 different colored stripes, and one with 10.

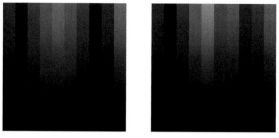

Stripe colors: 5
File size: 2.96 KB

Stripe colors: 10
File size: 3.14 KB

Figure 3-11. Comparing the file size difference between PNGs with 5 or 10 colors.

These images were exported as PNG-24 images via the Save for Web tool in Photoshop. By increasing the number of colors in the image, we increased the file size by 6%. If you can find ways to decrease the number of colors in your image, perhaps by normalizing the colors used in your site (as we'll cover in "Creating Repurposable Markup"), you can save file size, which will have a positive effect on performance.

In Figure 3-12, we're exporting the same file as in the initial PNG-8 example with transparency (Figure 3-9), but you'll notice that the transparency in the PNG-24 file is handled very differently.

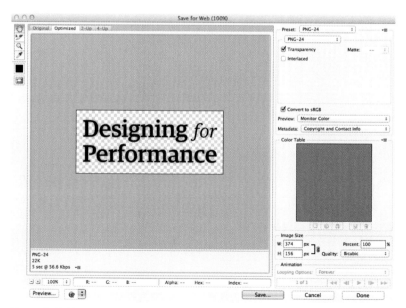

Figure 3-12. Transparent PNG-24 Export view.

In the PNG-8 file, Photoshop was working with a matte color to blend the drop shadow; there was no partial transparency, only fully transparent pixels beyond the drop shadow. In the PNG-24 file, we see partial transparency. This naturally results in a larger file size; the file size will also increase substantially in more complex images. If you don't need the transparency but have lots of colors in your image, choose JPEG instead.

There are some other tools that can give you partial transparency in PNG-8s, such as Fireworks (an image editing tool like Photoshop) and pngquant (a lossy compression tool for PNG images). However, if you need partial transparency when exporting an image from Photoshop, you'll want to use PNG-24. As always, run every image exported from Photoshop through an additional compression tool (read more in "Additional Compression").

It's important to note that older browsers, such as Internet Explorer 6, have limited support for PNGs. If you have enough traffic from older browsers that you need to optimize for them, be sure to test any exported PNGs to make sure they render as expected.

What About Newer Image Formats?

Newer image formats like WebP (*https://developers.google.com/speed/webp/*), JPEG XR (*http://en.wikipedia.org/wiki/JPEG_XR*), and JPEG 2000 (*http://en.wikipedia.org/wiki/JPEG_2000*) are further optimized for performance. As they gain traction with browsers and image creation software, we may have more opportunities to use these newer formats and further optimize our sites' images for page speed and perceived performance.

ADDITIONAL COMPRESSION

Before you export an image, make sure that you are exporting it only at the maximum pixel width and height that you need for the image. Serving an image that is larger than necessary and scaling it down within an image tag will negatively impact your page load time, as you are forcing the user to download more bytes than needed. Read more about how to handle serving the correct image size in "Deliberately Loading Content."

After you've exported the image, run it through a tool like ImageOptim (*http://www.imageoptim.com/*) or Smush.it (*http://www.smushit.com/*), which find the best compression technique for a variety of file types.

ImageOptim is software available for download for Macs. Drag and drop an image into ImageOptim, and watch it find the best *lossless* compression for your image and remove unnecessary color profiles and comments (see Figure 3-13). This software currently includes a number of existing compression tools, such as PNGOUT, Zopfli, Pngcrush, AdvPNG, extended OptiPNG, JpegOptim, jpegrescan, jpegtran, and Gifsicle. ImageOptim's optimization works on JPEGs, PNGs, and even animated GIFs by choosing the best compression methods for your image. Because ImageOptim uses lossless compression methods, the end result is a smaller file size without sacrificing quality, which is exactly what we aim for when optimizing for web performance.

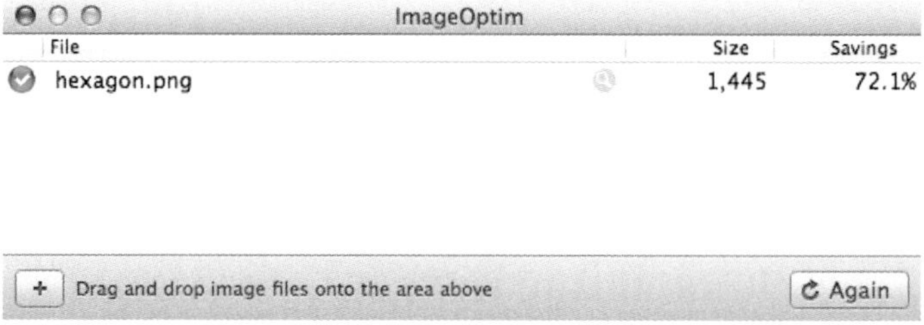

File	Size	Savings
hexagon.png	1,445	72.1%

Figure 3-13. ImageOptim is software that uses lossless compression methods to find savings in your image files.

Smush.it is also a lossless compression tool. It lives on the Web rather than on your desktop. Just like ImageOptim, it can process JPEGs, PNGs, and GIFs. The compression tools included in Smush.it are ImageMagick, pngcrush, jpegtran, and Gifsicle. Once you upload your image or choose its URL, Smush.it will choose the best compression method for it and then display a table with links to downloadable, compressed versions of your images (see Figure 3-14).

Smushed **54.50** or **2.75 KB** from the size of your image(s).
How did we do it? See the table below for more details.

Download Smushed Images

Smushed Images

Image ▲	Result	Source size	Result size	Savings	% Savings
b5922896%2Fhexagon.png	b5922896%2Fsmush%2Fhexagon.png	5.05 KB	2.30 KB	2.75 KB	54.50%

Figure 3-14. Smush.it is an online tool that uses lossless compression methods to find savings in your image files.

These tools can save you a ton of additional file size by finding ways to reduce the image size without reducing the quality of the image. In terms of weighing aesthetics and performance, running every image through one of these tools before uploading to the Web is a huge win.

If possible, automate the image optimization of any images uploaded to your website. You may have multiple content authors whose work-flow shouldn't be interrupted by the need to optimize individual images. Integrate tools like ImageOptim-CLI (*https://github.com/JamieMason/ImageOptim-CLI*) or WordPress plug-ins like EWWW Image Optimizer (*http://bit.ly/1ttTF1t*) into your site's build process to ensure that any new images created and uploaded will still get the additional compression they need.

Replacing Image Requests

In addition to decreasing your images' file sizes, it's also important to decrease the number of image requests on the page to improve page load time (read more about the basics of page load time in Chapter 2). Being deliberate about how you are requesting and loading images on your site will help you optimize both the total page load time and how quickly your users can begin to see and interact with your site. There are two main ways to eliminate image requests:

- Combine images into sprites

- Replace image files with CSS3, data URIs, or SVG versions

SPRITES

A common saying in the world of web performance is "the fastest request is a request not made." One way to reduce the number of image requests on your page is to combine images into sprites. Your page weight will increase slightly because you'll have one large image file and additional CSS to position and show the graphics within the image, but it's likely that combining images into a sprite will be a win for your site's page speed.

The best candidates for sprited images are small, repeated images incorporated into your site design. This may include icons, the site logo, and other CSS background images that are used around your site. Figure 3-15 is an example of a sprite.

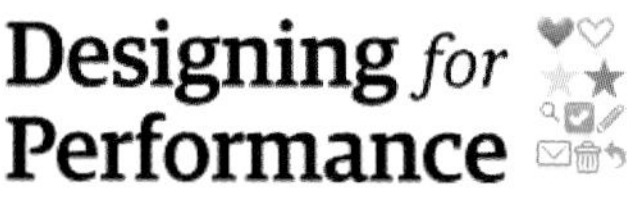

Designing *for* ♥♡ ★✩ Performance ⚪🗹✎ ✉🗑↩

Figure 3-15. This example sprite.png file contains a logo and heart, star, and other icons that we can use throughout a site's design.

You can see that this sprite includes a main logo as well as various versions of stars and other icons. Let's implement parts of this sprite using CSS and HTML. Figure 3-16 shows what we want the output to look like.

Designing *for* Performance

☆ We have a favorite!

★ We have a winner!!

Figure 3-16. This screenshot shows how we want our sprite to be used on the page.

Without a sprite, we have individual images applied to each element. Here is our starter markup:

```
<h1>Designing for Performance</h1>
<p class="fave">We have a favorite!</p>
<p class="fave winner">We have a winner!!</p>
```

In this HTML, we are going to apply the logo to the h1 element, one of the stars to the first paragraph with the class fave, and a different class to the paragraph with the additional class of winner. Here is our starter CSS with each individual image applied:

```css
h1, .fave:before {
    background: transparent no-repeat;  ❶
}

h1 {
    background-image: url(h1.png);
    text-indent: -9999px;  ❷
    height: 75px;
    width: 210px;
}

.fave {
    line-height: 30px;
    font-size: 18px;
}

.fave:before {  ❸
    background-image: url(star.png);
    display: block;
    width: 18px;
    height: 17px;
    content: '';
    float: left;
    margin: 5px 3px 0 0;
}

.winner:before {
    background-image: url(star-red.png);
}
```

1. We are applying a transparent background-color to these elements, and we're telling it to not repeat the background-image across the entire width and height of the elements.

2. We use text-indent to move the text within the h1 off the visible area of the page and to allow the background-image to show through. There are a number of ways to move text off the visible section of the page but still make it available to screen readers; you can also try the following method for hiding visible text:

```css
element {
    text-indent: 100%;
    white-space: nowrap;
    overflow: hidden;
}
```

This `text-indent:` `100%` method may also significantly increase performance on the iPad 1 in cases where you are applying many animations to this element.

3. To get the star to show up to the left of the paragraph text, I'm applying the image to the `:before` pseudoelement for the paragraph. The `:before` selector creates a new, inline element so you can insert content before the content of the selected element. `:after` is also a psuedoelement you can use. These pseudoelements are supported in modern browsers, with partial support in Internet Explorer 8 and no support in earlier versions of Internet Explorer.

Let's change this over to use a sprite instead of individual images. We'll use the preceding example sprite (Figure 3-15) and apply it to the h1 and `.fave:before` elements:

```
h1, .fave:before {
    background: url(sprite.png) transparent no-repeat;
}
```

Figure 3-17 shows what our new paragraph styling looks like with the sprite applied to the `:before` element.

Designing *for* Performance

⊤ We have a favorite!

⊤ We have a winner!!

Figure 3-17. This screenshot shows our paragraphs with the sprite applied to the before element, but without proper placement.

Now we need to determine the new `background-position` of our sprite so that the stars appear. The h1 received the default `background-position` of `0` `0`, or the top left of the sprite. `background-position` can accept different kinds of value pairs that correspond to the x-axis and y-axis, respectively:

- `50% 25%`

- `50px 200px`

- `left top`

In our case, we know where in the sprite our star images are, so we can use pixels to move the background-image over until each star shows. For the first star, we need to move the sprite 216px to the left and 15px up to show the sprite in our :before pseudoelement. We'll apply the following CSS to .fave:before in addition to its existing styles:

```
.fave:before {
    ...
    background-position: -216px -15px;
}
```

Our second star will automatically receive all of the styles we applied to the first, as both paragraphs share the class fave. We just need to choose a new background-position to show the red star icon:

```
.winner:before {
    background-position: -234px -15px;
}
```

Here's our final CSS with the sprite applied instead of individual images:

```
h1, .fave:before {
    background: url(sprite.png) transparent no-repeat;
}

h1 {
    text-indent: -9999px;
    height: 75px;
    width: 210px;
}

.fave {
    line-height: 30px;
    font-size: 18px;
}

.fave:before {
    display: block;
    width: 18px;
    height: 17px;
    content: '';
    float: left;
    margin: 5px 3px 0 0;
    background-position: -216px -15px;
}

.winner:before {
    background-position: -234px -15px;
}
```

Sprites can save a ton of page load time thanks to the decreased number of image requests. You'll notice that total page weight may increase with sprites due to the larger sprite image file size as well as additional CSS to use the sprite. However, using the sprite has a much better chance of a faster page load time than using individual images, as the browser has to fetch only one image rather than make lots of additional HTTP requests.

I created two pages on my site to test this example: one before we combined these images into a sprite, and one after. I ran them through WebPagetest to get a feel for the performance that a user may experience in each version (see Figure 3-18). Note that for any example like this, total load time and overall speed will vary between each test, but this gives us a rough estimate of the potential performance impact of sprites.

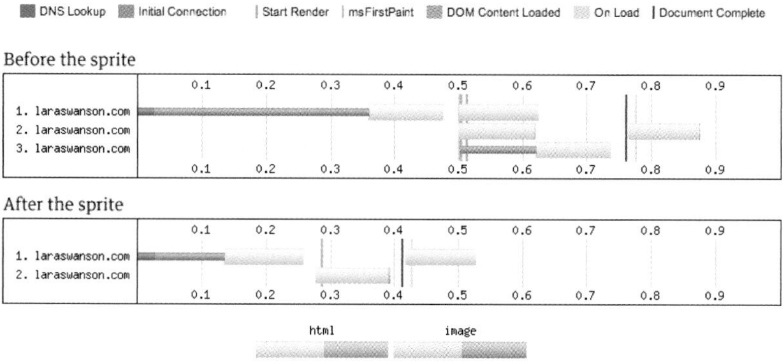

Figure 3-18. Connection view for our page before and after the sprite.

Figure 3-18 shows the connection view for our page before and after the sprite. Before the sprite, Chrome made three connections to retrieve the contents of the page. In the first connection, after the DNS lookup and initial connection, the browser grabbed the HTML for the page and then retrieved the first image. In the third connection, there is an initial connection time and then more image downloading. The last image to be downloaded (notice it begins in the second connection around document complete) is a favicon for the site.

After the sprite, Chrome made two connections to retrieve the contents of the page. In this connection, after the DNS lookup and initial connection, the browser retrieved the HTML and then the single sprite. Again, after document complete, the browser gets the favicon for the site. As you can see, document complete happens faster with the sprite than without it. Another way to visualize how much faster the sprited version feels is to look at the Speed Index metric (Figure 3-19).

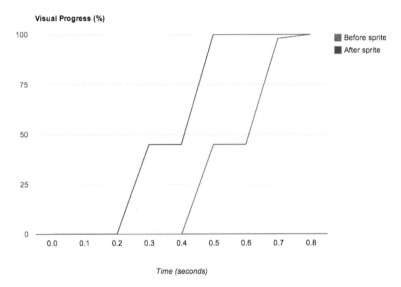

Figure 3-19. WebPagetest's Speed Index metric helps illustrate when a page becomes visually complete. WebPagetest calculates Speed Index by figuring out how "complete" the page is at various points in time during the page load, shown over time in this visual progress graph.

As mentioned in "Critical Rendering Path," Speed Index is the average time at which visible parts of the page are displayed. It's an excellent metric to watch as you try to measure the perceived performance of your page, as it will tell you how quickly the "above the fold" content is populated for your users. In this example, our graph of visual progress (from which Speed Index is calculated) shows how much faster the page appears visually complete over time with the sprite.

What About HTTP/2?

HTTP/2 is a major revision of the Web's protocol that is currently being defined. Its focus is to help improve performance, and one of the major chief goals of HTTP/2 is to allow the use of a single connection from a browser to a server, helping to optimize how browsers request assets. With HTTP/2, web servers hosting your site's files could hint or even push content back to your user's browser instead of waiting for it to request individual page assets. This means that the need for spriting could be eliminated in the future!

There are some potential performance downsides to using sprites, however. If you need to change one image within the sprite, you'll have to break the cache of the entire file. Also, by using the sprite you are forcing your users to download potentially unnecessary bytes; if the other icons in the sprite are never seen during a user's visit to your site, the user will have downloaded and decoded the larger file size for no reason. Consider these drawbacks when creating your sprite and measuring its performance impact.

In one experiment my team ran, we had a small section of a page that featured 26 thumbnail images rotating in and out of 10 slots. We combined all 26 images into a sprite, which:

- Increased the total page size by 60 KB due to the added CSS, JavaScript, and new image file needed to re-create this effect

- Decreased the number of requests by 21%

- Decreased the total page load time by 35%

These results demonstrate that it's worth experimenting with page load time optimizations. We weren't originally sure whether this technique would be an overall page speed win, but we knew it was worth an experiment so we could learn from it. Read more about measuring and iterating on performance wins in Chapter 6.

CSS3

Another way to decrease image requests is to replace them with CSS. You can create shapes, gradients, and animations using CSS. For example, CSS3 gradients:

- Can handle transparency
- Can be overlaid on a background color
- Eliminate an image request
- Are super easy to change

CSS can be a great, performant replacement for images. Don't worry about the extra page weight from the vendor prefixes in CSS3 syntax; if you aren't already, you should be using gzip on your site (read more about how to implement and optimize for gzip in "Minification and gzip"), which will take care of optimizing this code. Even though you will be loading more CSS, it'll likely be a better-performing option than an image request.

One great place where CSS can replace images is a basic repeating gradient. Why use an image when you could use a simple, repurposable CSS3 gradient that eliminates an image request?

For example, you can create a single gradient that fades from white to transparent, and use this gradient on any element that you'd like to show with a bevel. Let's try this on three buttons:

```
<a href="#">Click Me</a>
<a href="#" class="buy">Buy This</a>
<a href="#" class="info">More Info</a>
```

In our CSS, we will have already applied font and spacing styles to these buttons. To add the basic bevel gradient:

```
a {
  background-image:
    linear-gradient(to bottom, #FFF, transparent);
  background-color: #DDD;
  border: 1px #DDD solid;
}
```

[NOTE]

In this example, I'm including only the W3C gradient syntax. You'll need to add syntaxes for other browsers, such as Firefox and Internet Explorer.

Based on this CSS, all of our links will have a gray background color, and overlaid on this background color will be our CSS3 gradient, applied as a background image. Each link also has a solid gray 1px border. To make the Buy This button green, and the More Info button blue, we simply change the background color and border color of each:

```
.buy {
  background-color: #C2E1A9;
  border-color: #D8E5CE;
}

.info {
  background-color: #AFCCD3;
  border-color: #DAE9EC;
}
```

The resulting buttons (Figure 3-20) will each have their own background color with a white-to-transparent gradient overlaid on top.

Click Me   Buy This   More Info

Figure 3-20. Buttons with CSS3 gradient backgrounds.

Using a gradient like this eliminates the need for an image request, which is excellent news for your page load time. You can do some pretty amazing things with CSS3 gradients because of the control they offer over where colors begin and end. Here is an example hexagon built for WebKit browsers using CSS3 gradients. We need only one element, so in this case I chose to use a div:

```
<div class="hexagon"></div>
```

Here is the corresponding CSS to turn this div into a colorful hexagon in WebKit browsers:

```
.hexagon {
  width: 333px; height: 388px;
  background-image:
    -webkit-linear-gradient(120deg, #fff 83px, transparent 0,
        transparent 419px, #fff 0),
    -webkit-linear-gradient(-120deg, #fff 83px, transparent 0,
        transparent 419px, #fff 0),
    -webkit-linear-gradient(160deg, transparent 345px,
        #1e934f 0),
    -webkit-linear-gradient(140deg, transparent 376px,
        #1e934f 0),
    -webkit-linear-gradient(120deg, transparent 254px,
        #085b25 0),
```

```
        -webkit-linear-gradient(150deg, #053b17 183px,
            transparent 0),
        -webkit-linear-gradient(80deg, transparent 96px,
            #085b25 0);
    background-color: #053b17;
}
```

Figure 3-21 shows how the hexagon renders in Chrome.

Figure 3-21. Hexagon made using only CSS3 gradients, inspired by Geometry Daily #286 (*http://bit.ly/1ttUnvu*).

To get started writing CSS3 gradients, check out tools like ColorZilla's Gradient Editor (*http://www.colorzilla.com/gradient-editor/*). You can play with different colors, the direction of the gradients, and which browsers you'd like to support. Let's try a cross-browser gradient that goes from top to bottom, starting at a light green and switching at the halfway point to a dark green. In this case, we're intentionally creating a hard stop between the two greens, rather than a smooth transition between the two.

Let's start with our fallback color, which would be applied to the **background** or **background-color** property of our element:

```
/* Old browsers should get a fallback color */
background: #7AC142;
```

I recommend setting a **background-color** for each element that has a gradient applied, so in the case where a CSS3 gradient isn't supported, you still may have a readable contrast between the text and the background of the element. Be sure to test gradients across browsers to make sure they are working as expected, and that any text is still readable.

To support more browsers, you'd apply the following CSS to the background or background-image property of the element:

```
/* FF3.6+ */
-moz-linear-gradient(top, #e4f3d9 50%, #7ac142 0);

/* Chrome, Safari4+ */
-webkit-gradient(linear, left top, left bottom,
    color-stop(0%,#e4f3d9), color-stop(50%,#e4f3d9),
    color-stop(51%,#7ac142));

/* Chrome10+, Safari5.1+ */
-webkit-linear-gradient(top, #e4f3d9 50%, #7ac142 0);

/* Opera 11.10+ */
-o-linear-gradient(top, #e4f3d9 50%, #7ac142 0);

/* IE10+ */
-ms-linear-gradient(top, #e4f3d9 50%, #7ac142 0);

/* W3C */
linear-gradient(to bottom, #e4f3d9 50%, #7ac142 0);
```

In the preceding syntax, the light green will start at the top of the element and continue to stay light green until 50% down the height of the element. To create the hard stop between the two greens, we can set 0 as our second color stop for many of the browsers' syntax. This indicates to the browser that the new color should start right away, after our 50% light green color stop. In the older Chrome and Safari syntax, however, we need to set multiple color stops and percentages to make sure it does what we want!

The resulting gradient will look like Figure 3-22.

Figure 3-22. CSS3 gradient with a hard stop.

background Versus background-image

What's the difference between applying a gradient to a background instead of a background-image? Browsers are smart enough to know that when you declare a gradient for background, it should be applied as a background-image. The gradient will play nicely and not be overridden by any background-color declarations for the element. Your background-image will overlay the background-color declared. However, if you apply just a background declaration later in your CSS to an element with a background-image gradient, the new background declaration will override your gradient.

To support CSS3 gradients in older versions of Internet Explorer, you need to apply a `filter` property to the element. However, we can create only a smooth gradient using the `filter` property; we will be missing out on the hard color stop between our two greens:

```
/* IE6-9 */
filter: progid:DXImageTransform.Microsoft.gradient(
   startColorstr='#e4f3d9',endColorstr='#7ac142',
   GradientType=0 );
```

You should analyze the visitor traffic for your site to determine which browser versions you need to support with vendor prefixes.

The preceding CSS also includes the W3C standard for gradients: `linear-gradient`. Hopefully in the future, as more browser vendors come to agreement on CSS3 gradient syntax, we can clean up existing vendor prefixes from our CSS.

In addition to using CSS3 to create gradients, you can use CSS as a powerful image replacement tool in other areas: loading indicators, tool tips, and a variety of other simple graphics. There are plenty of examples on the Internet for CSS-only spinners (*http://dabblet.com/gist/7615212*), various shapes made with CSS (*https://css-tricks.com/examples/ShapesOfCSS/*), and repeating patterns using just CSS (*http://lea.verou.me/css3patterns/*).

That being said, be careful how your CSS affects repaint times, as there can be a cost to using a lot of CSS3. A repaint is an expensive operation performance-wise and can make your page look sluggish. If you find that your user interface does become sluggish, especially upon scrolling, you may have a CSS3 or JavaScript repaint issue and will want to diagnose what's causing it using tools from JankFree.org (*http://jank-free.org/*). Read more about this topic in "Perceived Performance."

DATA URIS AND BASE64-ENCODING IMAGES

Replacing very small, simple images with data URIs is also a way to decrease the number of requests a web page has to make. To do this, change an image to a URI by converting it to text using a method called *Base64 encoding*. For example, let's say we have a PNG-8 image of a small triangle (Figure 3-23) that we want to reuse in various places across a site.

◹

Figure 3-23. Small triangle in PNG-8 format.

We can convert the image to its text equivalent (a data URI) using an online Base64 encoder. We upload our image and the encoder returns a data URI for us to use in our CSS. The result of Base64-encoding this triangle and applying it to the background-image of an element using CSS would look like this:

```
background-image: url(data:image/png;base64,iVBORwOKGgoAAAANSUh
EUgAAAAoAAAAQCAAAAAAKFLGcAAAAVU1EQVR4AWM4/B8GGOyfw5m6UQimx3
Y4c6PKTxjzUn4FnPmB7QaM+X+CDZz5P2E+nHlS6C2M+b86Ac78b3MYzlyq8
hPG/J/fAmSegQC22wzhx1BQAQBbjnsWelX9QwAAAABJRU5ErkJggg==);
```

Using Base64 to encode images saves an HTTP request by embedding the code for the image, which is generally a good rule of thumb for performance. It allows the image to be processed and display the image immediately rather than wait for the HTTP request for the image.

However, inlining images also removes your ability to cache the file, and it also makes your CSS larger (sometimes substantially, depending upon the length of the data URI). Be sure to measure the performance consequences of changing any images to data URIs before permanently implementing them on your site to make sure they're actually a performance win for you.

SVG

Some icons and images are great candidates for replacement with *scalable vector graphics* (SVG). If you have a single-color or gradient image, transparency, or very little detail in your graphic, consider exporting it as an SVG. SVG uses XML to define basic properties of the image using paths, shapes, fonts, and colors.

The major advantage of using SVG images is that both nonretina and retina devices will display them beautifully. Rather than creating high-resolution duplicates of your images to serve up to high-resolution displays, you can replace them with SVGs. SVGs will appear at the right size and definition because they are vectors that scale smartly, unlike raster images. Also, by replacing an image file with inline SVG, you are eliminating an HTTP request to go and fetch the file from the server.

SVGs are not supported on Internet Explorer 8 or lower, nor are they supported on devices running Android 2.x. However, SVG feature detection is reliable, so you can use tools to fall back from SVG images to PNG versions. For example, Grunticon (*https://github.com/filamentgroup/grunticon*) allows you to upload a set of SVG files and generates CSS for applying icons as SVG background images along with fallback PNG images and CSS.

To create an SVG image using Adobe Illustrator, choose File > Save As and under Format, choose SVG. This will create a new SVG file that you can edit using a text editor. You'll be given a number of export options (Figure 3-24).

Choose the following settings to create the simplest (and smallest) SVG file without compromising quality:

- *SVG Profiles:* SVG 1.1. This is a well-supported version of SVG.

- *Font Type:* SVG.

- *Subsetting:* None (Use System Fonts).

- *Images:* Embed. This will embed any bitmaps into the SVG rather than externally linking to them.

- *Preserve Illustrator Editing Capabilities:* Deselect. We don't need this functionality when using an SVG on our site.

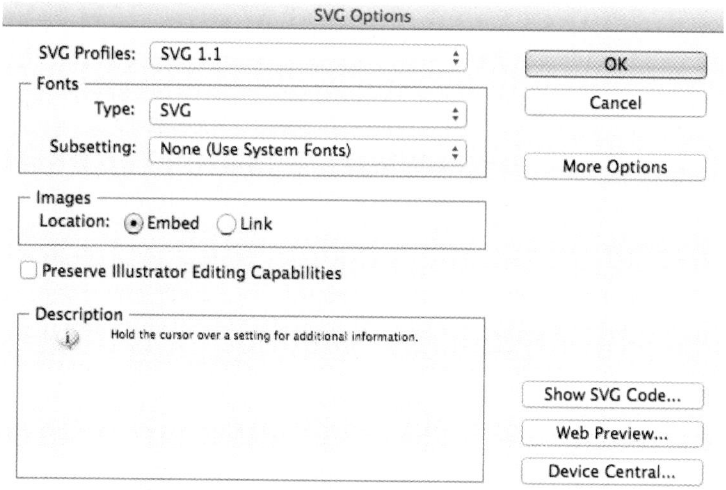

SVG Options

SVG Profiles: [SVG 1.1 ⟋⟍]   [OK]

Fonts
    Type: [SVG ⟋⟍]   [Cancel]

  Subsetting: [None (Use System Fonts) ⟋⟍]   [More Options]

Images
  Location: (•) Embed ◯ Link

☐ Preserve Illustrator Editing Capabilities

Description
    ⓘ   Hold the cursor over a setting for additional information.

[Show SVG Code...]

[Web Preview...]

[Device Central...]

Figure 3-24. SVG export options.

For this example, I've created a star SVG (Figure 3-25) using Adobe Illustrator.

Figure 3-25. Star in SVG format.

Open your SVG file in a text editor. In your saved SVG, all you'll need are a few XML tags, such as:

```
<svg>
  <path/>
</svg>
```

However, upon opening this star file in plain text, I can see that Adobe Illustrator passed through quite a bit of unnecessary code into our SVG:

```
<?xml version="1.0" encoding="utf-8"?>

<!-- Generator: Adobe Illustrator 15.0.2, SVG Export Plug-In .
  SVG Version: 6.00 Build 0)  -->

<!DOCTYPE svg PUBLIC "-//W3C//DTD SVG 1.1//EN"
  "http://www.w3.org/Graphics/SVG/1.1/DTD/svg11.dtd">

<svg version="1.1" xmlns="http://www.w3.org/2000/svg"
  xmlns:xlink="http://www.w3.org/1999/xlink" x="0px" y="0px"
```

```
width="20px" height="20px" viewBox="0 0 20 20"
enable-background="new 0 0 20 20" xml:space="preserve">

<polygon fill="#FFFFFF" stroke="#000000" stroke-miterlimit="10"
  points="10,2.003 11.985,8.112 18.407,8.112 13.212,11.887
  15.196,17.996 10,14.221 4.803,17.996 6.789,11.887 1.592,
  8.112 8.015,8.112 "/>

</svg>
```

Feel free to remove the following components from your exported SVG. They don't affect the output of your SVG file in a browser, and we should optimize for the smallest file size possible for performance:

- The `<!DOCTYPE>`... line

- The `<!-- Generator: Adobe Illustrator`... comment

- The `<?xml`... statement

You can also automate the cleanup of SVG files with tools like Scour (*http://codedread.com/scour/*) and SVGO (*https://github.com/svg/svgo*). Be sure to run this kind of cleanup only on your exported SVG, not on the original file.

There are a few ways to implement your SVG image on your site. You can apply the SVG to the source attribute of an image tag:

```
<img src="star.svg" width="83" />
```

Our wonderful SVG will crisply expand to the width you set for it. Rather than including an SVG in your main HTML document, you can also apply it as a background to an element using CSS:

```
.star {
  background: url(star.svg);
  display: block;
  width: 83px;
  height: 83px;
  background-size: 83px 83px;
}
```

Or you could inline the SVG into your HTML:

```
<body>

  <svg version="1.1" xmlns="http://www.w3.org/2000/svg"
    xmlns:xlink="http://www.w3.org/1999/xlink" x="0px" y="0px"
    width="20px" height="20px" viewBox="0 0 20 20"
    enable-background="new 0 0 20 20" xml:space="preserve">
```

```
<polygon fill="#FFFFFF" stroke="#000000" stroke-miterlimit="10"
   points="10,2.003 11.985,8.112 18.407,8.112 13.212,11.887
   15.196,17.996 10,14.221 4.803,17.996 6.789,11.887 1.592,
   8.112 8.015,8.112 "/>

</svg>

</body>
```

Some sites use SVG images, but rather than apply them using CSS or an image tag, they combine the SVG images into an icon font. Tools like IcoMoon (*http://icomoon.io/*) can help you build a custom font made up of your own SVG images. However, icon fonts are not supported across all browsers, and it can be much more difficult to create fallbacks for your images where icon fonts aren't supported. Further, individually applied icons can be additionally complicated by the line-height and font-size styles applied to your elements, and they can be a challenge for accessibility (*http://bit.ly/1ttVjQw*).

Using a font *does* make it easier to change the color of an icon, as you can just apply the color CSS declaration to the character. However, individual SVG images tend to be easier to work with, and you can control the color of inline SVGs with CSS as well using the fill CSS property.

Though SVG isn't supported in older browsers, the forward-friendliness of supporting retina devices and easy workflows for supporting older browsers—such as Grumpicon (*http://www.grumpicon.com/*) or Modernizr (*http://modernizr.com/*)—make SVG an excellent image replacement choice for improving the performance of your site. For additional optimization of SVG files, run them through a compression tool like SVG Optimiser (*http://bit.ly/1ttVlb0*), which simplifies decimals and removes unnecessary characters.

Replacing images with inline SVG has the same set of downsides as replacing images with data URIs: it can add more file size to your HTML and eliminates the opportunity to cache the file. Measure the performance impact of replacing any images with SVG on your site before committing to the SVG versions.

Image Planning and Iterating

Image efficiency on your site comes down to careful planning at the design stage. If you know up front how and where you're going to be using images across your site, you can plan for things like transparency, size, gradients, and how you can reduce the total number of image requests.

As a site evolves, or as the number of designers contributing to image creation and updating increases, your images directory may grow out of control. There are a few things you can try to keep the file size and number of images on your site optimized and maintained, including scheduling routine checks on image directories and the makeup of your page weight, creating a style guide, and mentoring other image creators on the importance of optimized images.

SCHEDULE ROUTINE CHECKS

Schedule a routine check for your site to see what images can be reused, combined, or re-exported in a different format. When you look in the main directory (or directories) for the images that make up your site design, ask yourself:

- Have any of these sprites been updated recently? Are there any outdated icons within the sprite that I can remove, or have new graphics been added that need to be optimized?

- With new browser technology, or as our audience begins to use more modern browsers, which of these images can be replaced with modern techniques like CSS3 or SVG, or new technology like `picturefill`?

- Are all of the new images created since I last checked in the ideal format? Are they as simple as possible, and have they been run through an additional compression tool?

- Are all of the images scaled to the correct height and width? Am I displaying any images at a smaller scale than they've been exported, which means I should re-export at the right size to eliminate unnecessary overhead?

Similarly, routinely check the page weight of your site. Note the makeup of your total page weight, including what percentage of the total page weight is due to images. If the page weight has increased by a significant amount, figure out why, and see where you can make file size improvements. Read more about how to measure and iterate on page weight and other performance metrics in Chapter 6.

CREATE STYLE GUIDES

Consider creating a style guide as a reference point for how images are used across your site, especially when it comes to icon meaning and sprite usage. It could include:

- An easy way to find which classes to apply to your HTML to show different icons

- Definitions of icon usage and meaning so that designers and developers are able to create a consistent user experience across pages, with the added gain of reusing existing images that are cached

- Examples of CSS gradients and other techniques used to improve the performance of your site so that others may repurpose it instead of adding their own, which can cause bloated CSS files

- A definitive guide to which browsers you need to support so that other designers and developers know which syntaxes they must include in their CSS as well as what to test

A style guide has many other benefits for page load time beyond image documentation. In "Style Guides," we will walk through why they're so useful and what else you can include in them.

MENTOR OTHER IMAGE CREATORS

You are likely not the only person creating and updating the images on your site. There may be other designers and developers who need to understand these techniques, and there may also be other content creators who are not as well versed in image creation methods.

Make sure that there are well-defined workflows for how new images appear on the site. If a designer or developer is responsible for adding images, make sure that part of his or her workflow includes finding a balance of aesthetics and performance by testing qualities and running images through additional optimization. As much as possible, automate image optimization so that image creators don't feel like they have a new, burdensome workflow.

It's important to share this knowledge with others who contribute to the site so that you are not a sole "performance cop" or "performance janitor." Helping others understand their impact on page load time will be as beneficial to your image directory as it will be to your stress level. Read more about empowering and incentivizing others to champion performance in Chapter 8.

Again, optimizing images is likely the biggest win for performance on your site. As you take a look at the images on your site, ask yourself:

- Can I save on file size by choosing a different image format?

- Have all of my images been run through an additional compression tool?

- Would I be better served with a CSS3 gradient, data URI, SVG file, or sprite?

- Is there any unnecessary noise or grain in my image, or is there another way I can reduce the total number of colors in my image?

- How can I make sure that new images added to my site are optimized?

Continue to focus on the balance of aesthetics and performance as you create your images (read more about finding this balance in Chapter 7). Sometimes you'll need to export a slightly larger image because it looks significantly better. Other times, you'll be able to gain huge page speed savings by repurposing colors and icons rather than creating new, only slightly different versions. The important part is to be deliberate with your image creation and make choices about performance as you go.

In the next chapter, we'll cover optimizing HTML and CSS. Just as with images, focusing on your markup's size and how it renders in your browser is imperative as you optimize page load time. We can clean our HTML and CSS, find ways to document and repurpose design patterns to keep things clean, and optimize the loading of these assets. Often, cleaning HTML and CSS leads to cleaner stylesheet images, too. As a designer, you are in a unique position to create high-performing, easily editable, and repurposable markup for your site.

[4]

Optimizing Markup and Styles

While images make up the majority of most sites' page weight, the HTML and CSS that call and implement these images also impact total page load time. The way that you structure and name your markup can help you keep your site maintainable and high performing; intentional organization of your CSS and design patterns will allow you to focus on repurposability and the meaning behind your site's look and feel. Keeping both your HTML and CSS clean and meaningful will result in a faster-loading site and a better overall user experience. In this chapter, we will cover best practices for loading HTML, CSS, fonts, and JavaScript on your site.

Cleaning Your HTML

Clean HTML is the foundation for a high-performing site. Though older sites tend to suffer from multiple designers or developers editing and adding to markup, even newer sites can benefit from a clean sweep—looking for embedded or inline styles, unused or unnecessary elements, and poorly named classes and IDs.

In Chapter 1, I mentioned that I was able to cut page load time in half for one site by simply cleaning up its markup and styles. I focused on killing bloated HTML and CSS, which resulted in smaller HTML, CSS, and stylesheet image file sizes.

When looking at your site's HTML, watch for:

- Embedded or inline styles that should be moved to a stylesheet

- Elements that have no need for special styling (unnecessary HTML elements, also known as "divitis" and covered in the next section)

- Old, commented-out code that can be removed

If a site has been edited by multiple developers or designers, there may be markup that seems unused or unnecessary. As sites age, outdated techniques, like using tables for layout, tend to live on without being cleaned or updated to newer best practices. Be ruthless when eliminating any superfluous or outdated HTML. There's rarely a good "just in case" reason for keeping unnecessary or convoluted markup; it's often better to kill it and know that, if you really need to, you can reference it in the future using version control.

DIVITIS

"Divitis" happens when you have lots of elements in your HTML that serve little purpose other than to help you style content. Often divitis happens when lots of div elements take the place of more meaningful, semantic HTML elements, but the mess can happen with any kind of HTML element:

```
<div>
  <div>
    <header>
      <div id="header">
        <h1><span>Site Name</span></h1>
      </div>
    </header>
  </div>
</div>
```

It's unclear why we have so many elements in the preceding example; maybe there's something fancy that happens with styling within the span; maybe those other divs are meaningful to the structure of the page. But this is definitely a sign that something is wrong and should be inspected with your markup. Usually divitis is an indicator that the code author was overwhelmed with the cascading nature of styles and wanted to try to override the look and feel of an element, and did so by adding extra parent elements to target with CSS.

Divitis should be eradicated in your markup. It adds bloat to both your HTML and your CSS, and by removing unnecessary elements you'll create a much more meaningful and straightforward hierarchy for your site. If possible, use HTML5 elements (such as header and article) to create a semantic hierarchy. It will be easier to see how you should write your CSS, and will illuminate opportunities for repurposable design patterns.

To eliminate divitis, take a look at the styles applied to the elements in the bloated area. See if it's possible to combine style declarations and apply them to the correct, semantic HTML elements to result in a better HTML hierarchy, such as:

```
<header>
  <h1>Site Name</h1>
</header>
```

Or simply:

```
<h1>Site Name</h1>
```

Sometimes, you'll need to retain some elements for layout and semantic structure, such as the header element in this example. But more often than not, inspecting and reducing the number of elements on your page will surprise you; thanks to the power of HTML5 and CSS, you'll be able to accomplish a lot with a solid, lightweight HTML hierarchy.

SEMANTICS

Semantic element names are those that represent the kind of content within the element. Good semantic element choices include representative HTML5 elements like header or nav, or class and ID names like login or breadcrumbs. Avoid nonsemantic names, like left or blue, which describe the look and feel of content to the user rather than the content's meaning.

Renaming elements to be more semantic will help you create better HTML structure for your page, and will also allow you to create design patterns for reuse across the site. For example, here's a nonsemantic HTML structure with a little bit of divitis thrown in:

```
<div class="right">
  <div id="form">
    <form>
      <p class="heading">Login</p>
      <p>
        <label for="username">Username:</label>
        <input type="text" id="username" />
      </p>
      <p>
        <label for="password">Password:</label>
        <input type="text" id="password" />
      </p>
      <input type="submit" value="Submit" />
    </form>
  </div>
</div>
```

Our styles for this sidebar and login form:

```css
form {
  background: #ccc;
}

.right {
  float: right;
  width: 200px;
}

#form form {
  border: 1px #ccc solid;
  background: yellow;
  padding: 10px;
}

.heading {
  font-weight: bold;
  font-size: 20px;
}
```

In this example, there's nothing particularly meaningful about the way that these elements are currently named; it'd be very easy to override the styles for .right elsewhere in a stylesheet and not realize that it affects other elements that are using this class name.

Also, it's not clear which of these styles are design patterns that could be repurposed throughout the site. In this CSS, we set a background for #form, and then override this background color later in our CSS for this particular login form. It's likely that we want this particular login form to stand out. Renaming and restructuring it to be more semantic will result in a much more understandable CSS file and potential design pattern:

```html
<div class="sidebar">
  <form id="login">
    <h2>Login</h2>
    <ul>
      <li>
        <label for="username">Username:</label>
        <input type="text" id="username" />
      </li>
      <li>
        <label for="password">Password:</label>
        <input type="text" id="password" />
      </li>
      <li><input type="submit" value="Submit" /></li>
    </ul>
```

```
    </form>
  </div>
```

We replaced the existing nonsemantic structure with a significantly more semantic structure and naming convention. We now have a sidebar, a clear and unique name for our form, and an unordered list to group the form elements together. While it results in slightly more CSS, this is actually a good thing for the overall cleanliness of our code:

```
form {
  background: #ccc;
}

form ul {
  list-style-type: none;
  padding: 0;
}

h2 {
  font-weight: bold;
  font-size: 20px;
}

.sidebar {
  float: right;
  width: 200px;
}

#login {
  border: 1px #ccc solid;
  background: yellow;
  padding: 10px;
}
```

As you can see, it's going to be easy to keep all unordered lists within standard forms on our site styled the same way. Similarly, a header (in this case an h2) within our login form should have the same styling as other sibling headers within our page. Our .sidebar styles are much less likely to be overridden by future edits to our stylesheet, and #login can retain its very unique styling. Though this adds a few more lines of CSS to our example, it will also likely result in a cleanup of the rest of our CSS file, as we could eliminate other styles that override the styling of forms and paragraphs made to look like headers.

Semantic naming allows you to maintain your HTML and CSS as it ages, as it is easier to read, test, and edit over time. Cleaner HTML and CSS typically create smaller files, which improve page load time, and also reduce the risk of page weight bloat as a site ages. Because they are more meaningful, semantic structures allow for more repurposability of designs and styles, which in turn creates a better end user experience.

ACCESSIBILITY

In addition to the editability and performance of semantic markup, clean HTML benefits users with accessibility needs. Semantic HTML makes the hierarchy of content meaningful for browsers, search engines, and screen readers. With new HTML5 tags like `post` and `aside`, and through the implementation of existing semantic structures like headings, paragraphs, and lists, content on the Web can become more accessible to everyone. Search engine bots and screen readers for the visually impaired are primarily looking at the HTML content of your page, rather than how it displays in a browser with CSS styles applied and JavaScript animations and interactivity running. The cleaner and more semantic your HTML is, the better the experience is for these users.

The Web Content Accessibility Guidelines (WCAG) provide more information on how to make your website accessible to people with disabilities. If you are using a clean and semantic HTML hierarchy, you are well on your way to making your site accessible. The World Wide Web Consortium (W3C) provides a full WCAG 2.0 (*http://www.w3.org/WAI/WCAG20/quickref/*) checklist to help you understand and meet all of the current WCAG requirements.

FRAMEWORKS AND GRIDS

There are plenty of helpful frameworks and grids on the Web that aid designers and developers who are looking to start a website but don't want to start from scratch. Bootstrap, HTML5 Boilerplate, and 960 Grid are examples of foundation CSS, HTML, and JavaScript that can help you kick-start a site design.

However, grids and frameworks come at a cost. Because they are designed to cover a large number of generic use cases, they will include plenty of things that you don't need on your site. This extraneous content can be a hindrance to your page load time rather than an aid to your development time; if you're not careful about how much is included as you start implementing a grid or framework, you could have a lot of unnecessary assets, markup, or styles loaded on your site.

Here are some styles included in the HTML5 Boilerplate framework. They'd be helpful styles for sites that include `dfn`, `hr`, or `mark` elements, but these lines could be eliminated on sites that don't use these elements:

```
/**
 * Address styling not present in Safari 5 and Chrome.
 */

dfn {
    font-style: italic;
}

/**
 * Address differences between Firefox and other browsers.
 * Known issue: no IE 6/7 normalization.
 */

hr {
    -moz-box-sizing: content-box;
    box-sizing: content-box;
    height: 0;
}

/**
 * Address styling not present in IE 6/7/8/9.
 */

mark {
    background: #ff0;
    color: #000;
}
```

If you really want to use a framework, be sure to clean out all of the extraneous material before your end user tries to load your site. Remember that grids and frameworks are likely not providing the semantic structure that we're aiming for, as they are generic and one-size-fits-all. Some, like HTML5 Boilerplate, give you custom build options that you should take advantage of, as shown in Figure 4-1.

As much as possible, clean up the naming and element structure of your pages after implementing an out-of-the-box framework or grid. There's no excuse for forcing your end users to load unnecessary styles, markup, or JavaScript.

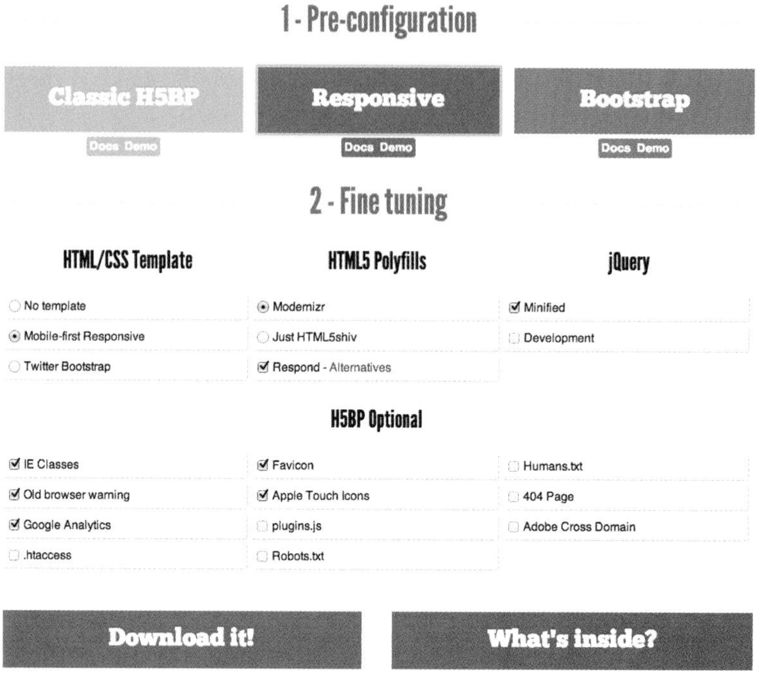

1 - Pre-configuration

Classic H5BP	Responsive	Bootstrap
Docs Demo	Docs Demo	Docs Demo

2 - Fine tuning

HTML/CSS Template	HTML5 Polyfills	jQuery
○ No template	◉ Modemizr	☑ Minified
◉ Mobile-first Responsive	○ Just HTML5shiv	☐ Development
○ Twitter Bootstrap	☑ Respond - Alternatives	

H5BP Optional

☑ IE Classes	☑ Favicon	☐ Humans.txt
☑ Old browser warning	☑ Apple Touch Icons	☐ 404 Page
☑ Google Analytics	☐ plugins.js	☐ Adobe Cross Domain
☐ .htaccess	☐ Robots.txt	

Download it!	What's inside?

Figure 4-1. Some frameworks give you custom build options before you implement them on your site, like in this HTML5 Boilerplate customization tool from Initializr (*http://www.initializr.com/*). Take advantage of these optimizations to reduce markup, styles, and script overhead.

Cleaning Your CSS

A thoughtful HTML hierarchy and deliberate choices about your site's layout and design will set you up for clean, easily editable, and performant CSS. As you examine your site's existing CSS to look for ways to clean it up, think about how it reflects your HTML hierarchy and design choices. Maybe you'll see:

- Element names that don't have semantic meaning
- !important declarations
- Browser-specific hacks
- Lots of selector specificity

Look for unused elements, styles that could be combined or rewritten for efficiency, and outdated ways of handling browser inconsistencies. As sites age, we need to routinely examine our CSS and consider implementing new technology and techniques to improve page load time. The more deliberate we can be with our site hierarchy and the purpose behind our design choices, the cleaner our CSS will be. Code maintainability and site performance go hand in hand.

UNUSED STYLES

If you have an existing site, the first CSS cleanup task to tackle is removing unused styles. As sites age, unused styles will crop up unnoticed, adding bloat to your stylesheets. Unused styles may be left over from deleted elements or entire pages on your site, elements that have been renamed or redesigned, or overrides from third-party widgets that you no longer use. There is no reason to keep unused selectors or styles in your stylesheets and force your end user to download them; your version control will come in handy should you ever need to look back in history to view old CSS.

There are a number of tools currently available to you for finding potential CSS to eliminate. Dust-Me Selectors (*http://www.brothercake. com/dustmeselectors/*) is a browser plug-in for Firefox and Opera that can scan your website's HTML to find unused selectors. In Chrome DevTools, there is an Audits tab (Figure 4-2) that will allow you to run a Web Page Performance audit and see a list of unused CSS rules.

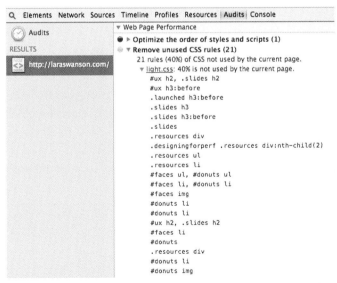

Figure 4-2. Chrome DevTools allows you to run a Web Page Performance audit on any page. Included in the audit results is a list of unused CSS rules that you may be able to clean up.

Be wary of the outputs of these tools; Dust-Me Selectors may not have crawled every page of your site, and Chrome DevTools is looking only at the CSS selectors on the current page (not any additional pages where the same stylesheet is called). These tools are excellent for helping you get an initial list of selectors to examine in your stylesheets and then begin to test removing them.

COMBINE AND CONDENSE STYLES

Duplicate styles for unique elements across your site are a great indicator of consistent styling and thoughtful design. Look through your stylesheets for opportunities to combine or condense these styles, as they will help with both the performance and maintainability of your code. Here we have two elements that share similar styles:

```css
.recipe {
  background: #f5f5f5;
  border-top: 1px #ccc solid;
  padding: 10px;
  margin: 10px 0 0;
  font-size: 14px;
}

.comment {
  background: #f5f5f5;
  border-top: 1px #ccc solid;
  padding: 10px;
  margin: 9px 0 0;
  font-size: 13px;
}
```

The only differences between the way these two elements are styled are that .comment has a different font-size declaration and margin declaration. We can combine these styles into one main declaration block and then style .comment's differences separately:

```css
.recipe, .comment {
  background: #f5f5f5;
  border-top: 1px #ccc solid;
  padding: 10px;
  margin: 10px 0 0;
  font-size: 14px;
}

.comment {
  margin: 9px 0 0;
  font-size: 13px;
}
```

Or, ask yourself: is there a reason why `.comment` has a slightly different font size and margin below it? What if you combined the styles in `.recipe` and `.comment` to create a true pattern? The complexity would be reduced and ease of maintenance would increase, and better yet, our CSS file will be shorter!

```
.recipe, .comment {
    background: #f5f5f5;
    border-top: 1px #ccc solid;
    padding: 10px;
    margin: 10px 0 0;
    font-size: 13px;
}
```

If you find that this pattern will be repeated often, you could also generalize the class name so it can be used throughout the site, rather than continuing to add class names to this comma-separated list.

Slight differences between elements that share a lot of styles could be due to many things: pixel-perfect web versions of PSD mockups, accidental updates to one place where a style existed but not another, and more. Throughout your stylesheets you may see many different pixel-specific heights, widths, margins, and padding defined. Are they intentionally slightly different from one another, or could they be normalized?

Look for these kinds of opportunities to normalize and create patterns. Presumably these elements share the same look and feel intentionally; as one element's design changes in the future, you'll probably want the other one to change in the same way. Combining them to define their shared styles will help save you development time in the future, and the shorter CSS file will help you with page load time now.

Additionally, you could begin to define rules for spacing and font sizes that are easy to follow. One great way to make these decisions easier is to look at your base `font-size` and use it to inform the rest of your design decisions. If your main content is a 14 px font with a `line-height` of 1.4 em, you could do a little math to create:

- Header font sizes in multiples of 14 px
- Margins and padding in multiples of 1.4 em
- A custom grid based on 14 px or 1.4 em increments

CSS also allows you to leverage the power of shorthand style declarations. Shorthand declarations, such as background, include many individual style values in one line. The background declaration, for example, includes:

- background-clip

- background-color

- background-image

- background-origin

- background-position

- background-repeat

- background-size

- background-attachment

You may set one, some, or all of these values when using background. Leveraging shorthand declarations like this allows you to further combine and condense styles in your CSS. For example, let's say we have three similarly styled elements with slightly different borders and padding:

```css
.recipe {
  background: #f5f5f5;
  margin: 10px 0 0;
  border: 1px #ccc solid;
  padding: 10px 0;
}

.comment {
  background: #f5f5f5;
  margin: 10px 0 0;
  border: 1px #fff solid;
  padding: 10px 0 0;
}

aside {
  background: #f5f5f5;
  margin: 10px 0 0;
  border: 2px #ccc solid;
  padding: 10px 0;
}
```

We can set the shorthand property for the styles that are common between the elements, and later style the small differences using individual (longhand) properties:

```css
.recipe, .comment, aside {
  background: #f5f5f5;
  margin: 10px 0 0;
  border: 1px #ccc solid;
  padding: 10px 0;
}

.comment {
  border-color: #fff;
  padding-bottom: 0;
}

aside {
  border-width: 2px;
}
```

This allows us to write easily readable CSS. If we had redefined the shorthand border declaration again for .comment, it would have been harder to figure out which part of the border was different from our original style declaration. By using the longhand property, we can easily spot what part of the style we are changing. Shorthand properties can reduce the amount of lines in our CSS, which is good for performance.

Sometimes, renaming elements can help you combine and condense styles. Take a look at these similarly styled elements:

```css
h3 {
  color: #000;
  font-weight: bold;
  font-size: 1.4em;
  margin-bottom: 0.7em;
}

#subtitle {
  color: red;
  font-weight: bold;
  font-size: 1.4em;
  margin-bottom: 0.7em;
}

.note {
  color: #333;
  font-weight: bold;
  font-size: 1.4em;
  margin-bottom: 0.7em;
}
```

```
<h1>My page title</h1>

<article>
  <h2>My article title</h2>
  <div id="subtitle">My article's subtitle</div>
  <p>...</p>
</article>

<aside>
  <div class="note">I have a side note</div>
  <p>...</p>
</aside>

<footer>
  <h3>My footer also has a title</h3>
</footer>
```

In a case like this, it may be possible to rename elements to create a more semantic hierarchy as well as cleaner CSS. Use your best judgment. In this case, we'll decide that in fact #subtitle, .note, and h3 are all semantically third-level headers in our page and rename them in our HTML:

```
<h1>My page title</h1>

<article>
  <h2>My article title</h2>
  <h3>My article's subtitle</h3>
  <p>...</p>
</article>

<aside>
  <h3>I have a side note</h3>
  <p>...</p>
</aside>

<footer>
  <h3>My footer also has a title</h3>
</footer>
```

By renaming them in our HTML, we've automatically combined the original styles in our CSS, as they now all fall under the h3 style block. We can add specificity to change the colors of the article and aside headers below this block:

```
h3 {
  color: #000;
  font-weight: bold;
  font-size: 1.4em;
```

```
    margin-bottom: 0.7em;
}

article h3 {
  color: red;
}

aside h3 {
  color: #333;
}
```

Lastly, if you use a CSS preprocessor like LESS or SASS, you may still end up with a bloated CSS file with lots of opportunity for repurposing or condensing styles. Good planning and purposeful, reusable design patterns will help you develop CSS using a preprocessor, just like when you're writing regular CSS. Focus on keeping any *mixins* (reusable style blocks that are defined once) as efficient as possible, and be sure to watch the output of your stylesheets over time. Bloated files can sneak up on you, and it's good to routinely and continually check on your CSS efficiency.

CLEAN STYLESHEET IMAGES

Once you've combined and condensed styles, take a look at any images called from your stylesheet. Remember, images make up the majority of most sites' page weight, so reducing the size and number of stylesheet image requests will be a huge boost to your site's page load time.

First, look for opportunities to create sprites. If you have many icons or other small images used throughout the site, a sprite can be a huge help in optimizing requests. Read "Sprites" for more information on how sprites boost performance, and how to implement them.

Second, as sites age, so do their sprites. You may notice that existing sprites include outdated or no-longer-used images. Examine your existing sprites: are there any sections that can be removed? Can you clean up the CSS that uses these sections? Can you clean up and then re-export the sprite image in a more appropriate file type or with higher compression? The cleaner your sprites are, the better your page load time will be.

Next, look for opportunities to replace your stylesheet images with CSS3 gradients, data URIs, or SVG. You can read more about creating gradients in "CSS3," and more about how to create high-performing

SVG replacements in "SVG." CSS3 gradients are an excellent replacement for any repeating background images that are currently implemented with CSS; they are also very easily editable and repurposable throughout stylesheets. Replacing images with CSS3 may very quickly speed up your site. Similarly, replacing stylesheet images with SVG can improve your page load time, as an SVG file can replace both retina and nonretina images in your stylesheet.

Ensure that any new icons or other images added to your stylesheet have meaning or purpose in your site design. Document these in a style guide so that other developers or designers can see what icons have already been added to the site and how they are currently used. Often, stylesheet image creep occurs because it's unclear what images are already available for use across a site. I've seen many sites develop multiple ways to indicate warnings or alerts with various icons and highlighting, rather than stick with a single styling convention. As you examine your stylesheet to find opportunities for design patterns, consider the number of stylesheet images called and whether they can be condensed.

REMOVE SPECIFICITY

When it comes to CSS, *specificity* is the term for how you write out selectors to help a browser determine which CSS rules are applied. There are different kinds of selectors, and each carries its own weight; specificity is calculated by a formula (*http://bit.ly/1ttWQGk*) based on these selectors. If two selectors apply to the same element, the one with higher specificity wins.

You'll often see overly specific selectors in a CSS file. This usually occurs when a designer or developer was trying to add weight to override previously defined styles that apply to a certain selector. For example:

```
div#header #main ul li a.toggle { ... }
```

Why did this stylesheet author choose to add all of these selectors in a row? Why wasn't it possible to simply style:

```
.toggle { ... }
```

It's possible that the author really needed all of that specificity in order to set a style correctly. However, this much specificity is also an indicator that something in the stylesheet or HTML hierarchy could be much more efficient. Inefficient selectors tend to happen because of

CSS overriding previous overly specific CSS, and this is a good thing to watch for so you can find areas to clean up and make more efficient. This happens frequently in larger organizations where there are many people touching the same piece of code.

Inefficient selectors used to be considered inherently bad for performance, but that's less of a concern these days with high-performing modern browsers. However, it's still smart to clean up selectors, as they can help you maintain your frontend architecture.

The more efficient your CSS is, the better performing it will be. Reducing specificity means that it will be easier to override styles with the naturally cascading power of CSS, rather than slip in additional weight or !important rules. Inefficient selectors and !important rules tend to add bloat to CSS files. Always start with the smallest, lightest selector possible and add specificity from there.

Optimizing Web Fonts

Web fonts add more requests and page weight to your site. Fonts are the classic example of weighing aesthetics and page speed; it's important to focus on making fonts as efficient as possible, loading them deliberately, and measuring their impact on both performance and engagement metrics to make sure they're worth including.

Loading a web font looks like this:

```
@font-face {
  font-family: 'FontName';
        /* IE9 Compatability Mode */
  src: url('fontname.eot');
        /* IE6-IE8 */
  src: url('fontname.eot?#iefix') format('embedded-opentype'),
        /* Modern Browsers */
        url('fontname.woff') format('woff'),
        /* Safari, Android, iOS */
        url('fontname.ttf') format('truetype');
}
```

Support for the *Web Open Font Format*, or WOFF (*http://caniuse. com/#feat=woff*), is increasing, so depending upon your user base and which browsers your site supports, you may be able to move to a shorter @font-face declaration, which would support Chrome 6+, Firefox 3.6+, IE 9+, and Safari 5.1+:

```
@font-face {
  font-family: 'FontName';
  src: url('fontname.woff') format('woff');
}
```

You'll then apply this font to a selector using font-family, and include fallback fonts just in case your new font hasn't loaded for your user:

```
body {
  font-family: 'FontName', Fallback, sans-serif;
}
```

Why Include a Fallback Font?

There will be a small subset of visitors to your site whose browsers don't support web fonts, or who have disabled web font loading. There's also a chance that your font has broken or the browser can't find it. If the user's browser can't find the first font in a font-family list, it will try the second font, and so forth. Your fallback font list should contain one font that is similar to your primary font, at least one font that is available across platforms (like Georgia or Arial), and a generic font such as sans-serif or serif.

Web font files come in a range of sizes, from just a few kilobytes to upward of 200 kilobytes. Inspect your web font files to see how large they are and look for the following opportunities to cut their weight:

- Do you need only a few characters rather than the entire alphabet and all punctuation, such as when you're applying a font just to a logo?

- Does the font support multiple languages? Is it possible to reduce language support to just one subset (such as a Latin subset)?

- Can you eliminate any unnecessary individual characters?

Character subsetting is a powerful tool for reducing your web font file size. If you're using a font from a hosted font service such as Google, you may be able to choose to load only a certain character subset. In this example, we would load Google's Philosopher font with a Cyrillic subset:

```
<link href="http://fonts.googleapis.com/css?family=Philosopher
  &subset=cyrillic" rel="stylesheet" />
```

If you want to load only certain characters from a Google hosted font, you can specify those as well. For example, we can load the Philosopher font with only the characters *H*, *o*, *w*, *d*, and *y*:

```
<link href="http://fonts.googleapis.com/css?family=Philosopher
    &text=Howdy" rel="stylesheet" />
```

Externally hosted fonts like those from Google have a better chance of already being cached for your visitors, but if they're not cached for a particular visitor, then they'll require an extra lookup and request from the external domain to be fetched. Self-hosted fonts save that extra DNS lookup but will not be already cached the first time a visitor comes to your site.

One additional benefit of hosting the font yourself is customization of the font file. If you are hosting your own web font, you can run it through a tool like Font Squirrel's Webfont Generator (*http://www.fontsquirrel.com/tools/webfont-generator*) and choose a custom character subset to optimize the font file, as shown in Figure 4-3.

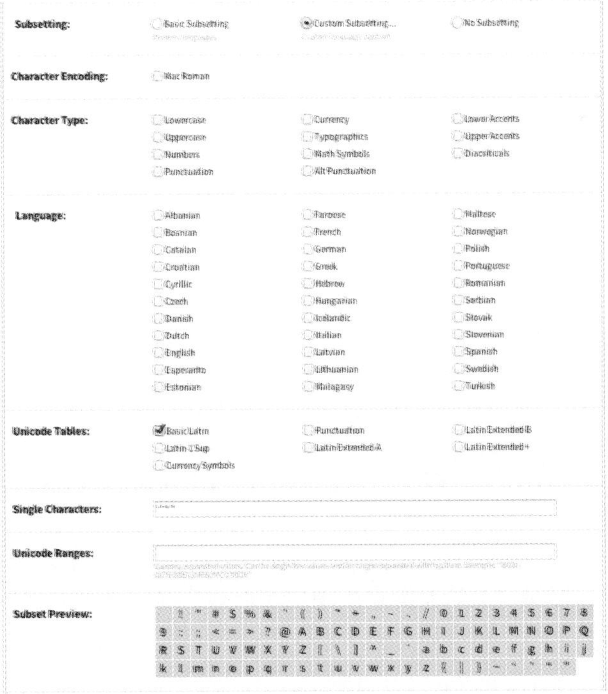

Figure 4-3. Font Squirrel's Webfont Generator allows you to choose a custom subset of characters in your font files. In this case, we've chosen the Basic Latin Unicode table and added four single characters to our subset.

You may also want to use multiple font weights for your web font. Be deliberate about how many font weights you load; as you apply more font files, the page will get heavier and will require more requests, which has a hugely negative impact on performance. Use as few alternative weights as possible, and be sure to weigh the balance between aesthetics and performance with fonts (read more about this choice and how to measure it in Chapter 7).

An additional optimization you can make to your web font loading technique is to load fonts only on large screens. This will eliminate the requests and extra page weight on smaller devices like smartphones, which tend to take larger performance hits (read more about why in "Mobile Networks"). Use a media query to apply the web font:

```
@media (min-width: 1000px) {
  body {
    font-family: 'FontName', Fallback, sans-serif;
  }
}
```

The most important action you can take when applying web fonts is to be deliberate about their uses. Document when and how to use a particular font weight so that others working on your site can repurpose this markup and understand when it is appropriate to apply a font weight. Make it clear that a particular display weight should be used only for a certain kind of header, or that you reserve a text weight for special design patterns. This will help educate other designers and developers working on your site, and hopefully will help keep your site as fast as possible. Read more about the performance benefits of creating style guides in "Style Guides."

Creating Repurposable Markup

Creating design patterns using repurposable markup is the key to maintaining performance as your site's design evolves. As you make decisions about the meaning of your site's hierarchy, layout, and feel, you have the opportunity to be deliberate about loading assets and creating opportunities for markup reuse across the site. Design patterns save both development time and page load time. Markup reuse will:

- Provide an opportunity for asset caching
- Prevent designers or developers from reinventing the wheel

- Eliminate unnecessary asset requests as new content is added

- Help you isolate styles and assets that are no longer necessary

By normalizing the colors used across the site, documenting reusable patterns like spinners and sprites, and defining when and how to implement assets like fonts, you can equip your team to make smart decisions about page load time as your site evolves.

Let's take normalizing colors as an example. Examine your site's CSS file and find all of the color values used. How many different shades of gray are implemented? When you show warning indicators in your user interface, do they use a consistent set of colors, or are there multiple shades of red or yellow? How about your main site colors: do you have a single hexadecimal value that is repeated throughout the site, or are there variations of lightness and saturation around a theme?

The more variation you have in colors throughout your design, the less meaningful those colors will be and the messier your stylesheet can become. Collect them all in one place and see which can be condensed. As you narrow down your color choices, start to determine why these colors may be used. For example, a List Apart's pattern library includes a description of when to use certain colors (Figure 4-4).

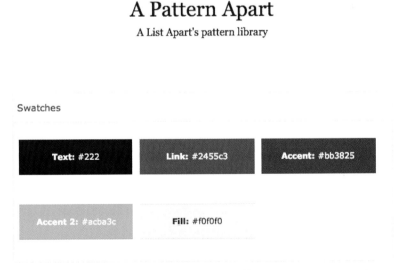

Figure 4-4. A List Apart's pattern library (*http://patterns.alistapart.com/*) includes a description of when to use certain colors.

When I worked on a site with lots of golden yellows and deep grays, I cleaned up the stylesheet to make the site's colors more consistent. I documented which hexadecimal code to use when a designer wanted to use a bold yellow, a light yellow, a red warning message, a green "changed" message, and so on. I also went through and cleaned up all gray usage, determining which values should be used and when (such as #aaa for disabled text and borders, #eee for backgrounds, etc.). After documenting the colors and their meaning, I went through and replaced existing colors with the new, normalized values. This allowed me to combine and condense many styles, since there were now repurposable patterns. These efforts decreased the main stylesheet file by 6%, saving not just future development and maintenance efforts, but also page load time.

STYLE GUIDES

Creating repurposable design patterns is excellent, and the key to their continued reuse is documentation. Style guides can be great resources for many audiences: editors, developers, designers, and anyone else who may look for guidance on your site's design and development best practices.

Style guides showcase the best way to implement code and request assets, allowing you to make sure other people who work on your site also are helping to make it as high performing as possible. Putting your site logo assets in one place and optimizing the files to be as small as possible and in the best format for the job will help ensure that future logo implementations also follow best practices. Documenting your site's standardized and optimized loading indicator will make it easy for a future designer to implement this pattern and not reinvent the wheel with a new, slow, heavy spinner. Putting effort into your style guide now will help ensure that your site remains as fast as possible in the future.

Consider including the following information in your style guide:

- Hexadecimal color values and when they should be used

- Button classes and how they should be used

- Sprites and what classes correspond to which icons within them

- Typography, including how headers should be styled and how to import and apply any web fonts

As you document best practices, include notes on how to implement these styles. Add example HTML or CSS markup, how to include the right JavaScript file, or any other notes on efficient implementation. For example, Yelp's style guide (*http://www.yelp.com/styleguide*) includes a section on buttons that showcases the right way to style primary, secondary, and tertiary buttons, as well as a section on deprecated button styles that should no longer be used (Figure 4-5).

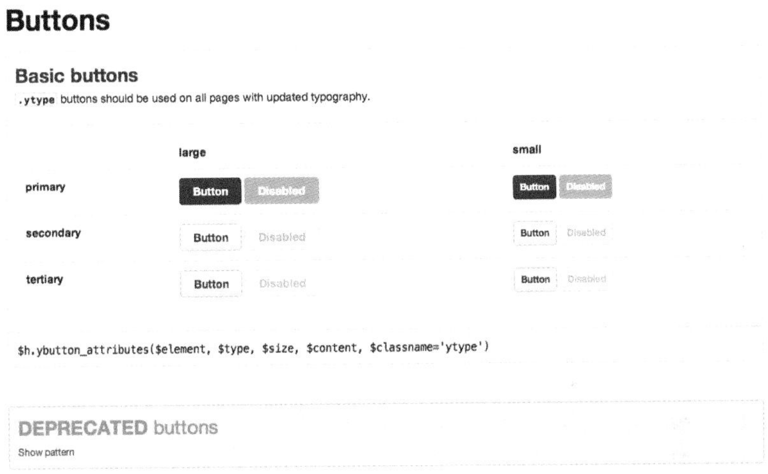

Buttons

Basic buttons

.ytype buttons should be used on all pages with updated typography.

	large		small	
primary	Button	Disabled	Button	Disabled
secondary	Button	Disabled	Button	Disabled
tertiary	Button	Disabled	Button	Disabled

$h.ybutton_attributes($element, $type, $size, $content, $classname='ytype')

DEPRECATED buttons
Show pattern

Figure 4-5. Yelp's style guide includes a section on buttons that showcases the right way to style primary, secondary, and tertiary buttons, as well as a section on deprecated button styles that should no longer be used.

Make any markup easy to copy and paste so that the barrier to excellent implementation is low for future designers and developers. For example, the Starbucks style guide (*http://www.starbucks.com/static/reference/styleguide/*) includes a how-to on implementing the company's icon font, with example HTML and CSS as well as embedded examples of each icon (Figure 4-6). It should be as easy and intuitive as possible to repurpose the patterns and reuse the assets in your style guide.

Video Player Icons

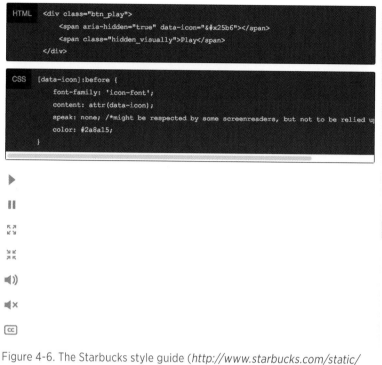

```
HTML    <div class="btn_play">
            <span aria-hidden="true" data-icon="&#x25b6;"></span>
            <span class="hidden_visually">Play</span>
        </div>
```

```
CSS     [data-icon]:before {
            font-family: 'icon-font';
            content: attr(data-icon);
            speak: none; /*might be respected by some screenreaders, but not to be relied u|
            color: #2a8a15;
        }
```

Figure 4-6. The Starbucks style guide (*http://www.starbucks.com/static/ reference/styleguide/*) includes a how-to on implementing the company's icon font, with example HTML and CSS as well as embedded examples of each icon.

A combination of easy-to-understand use cases, markup that can be copied and pasted easily, and beautiful examples will make it easy for other people working on your site to implement these patterns. Be thorough in your documentation while keeping it intuitive. For example, when documenting web font usage, outline the potential font weights you could include, how to implement each efficiently, and rules about when they should be used, like we did in Etsy's style guide (Figure 4-7).

Repurposable patterns save page load time as well as design and development time. As your site's design changes in the future, it will be even easier to update all the instances of a particular pattern, because they will share the same assets and styles. The more patterns are repurposed, the higher the chances are that the styles and other assets will already be cached, the shorter your stylesheets will be, and the faster the site will load.

Typography

There are two main types of Guardian fonts available for use: those for display, and those for text. The Guardian display and text weights can be applied to any element type (h1 , p , etc.). Please be judicious when including font files; some browsers download all @font-face files referenced in a CSS file, regardless of whether or not the font is actually applied to an element on the page. Only @import the font weight/style necessary to your design.

Guardian Weight	Appearance	Markup
	Display weights should be used for title and promo copy at sizes no less than 18px.	

Display Light	Lorem ipsum sit amet	`@import "/fonts/guardian-egyptt-light.css";`
		
		`.your-element {`
		`    font-family: "Guardian-EgypTT", Georgia, serif;`
		`    font-weight: 300;`
		`}`

Display Regular	Lorem ipsum sit amet	`@import "/fonts/guardian-egyptt-regular.css";`
		
		`.your-element {`
		`    font-family: "Guardian-EgypTT", Georgia, serif;`
		`    font-weight: 400;`
		`}`

Figure 4-7. Etsy's style guide includes example @font-face weights, instructions for when to use various fonts, and copy-and-pasteable code for CSS implementation.

Additional Markup Considerations

After you've cleaned up your markup and styles, there are additional optimizations you can make to your assets' load order, minification, and caching to improve page load time. Deliberately loading assets and understanding how they are delivered to your user will help you improve your site's overall user experience.

CSS AND JAVASCRIPT LOADING

There are two main rules when it comes to loading CSS and JavaScript:

- Load CSS from the <head>.
- Load JavaScript at the bottom of the page.

Now that you've read about the critical rendering path in "Critical Rendering Path," you know that CSS blocks rendering. If stylesheets are included near the bottom of the page, they will prohibit the page from displaying its content as soon as possible. Browsers want to avoid having to redraw elements of the page if their styles are changing; putting your stylesheets in the <head> allows content to be displayed progressively to the user because the browser isn't still looking for more style information.

Reducing your stylesheets to as few files as possible will help reduce the total number of requests your site makes, and will result in a much faster page load time. This also means you should avoid using @import, which can significantly increase page load time. Smaller CSS is always better; I recommend aiming for 30 KB or less of CSS and a single stylesheet wherever possible. For larger sites, it can be better to have one sitewide stylesheet and then page-specific stylesheets as needed. This way, the sitewide stylesheet is cached and the user will need to download only a little bit of additional CSS for each page with additional styles.

JavaScript files should be loaded at the end of the page and loaded asynchronously whenever possible. This will allow other page content to be displayed to the user more quickly, as JavaScript blocks DOM construction unless it is explicitly declared as asynchronous.

When a browser's HTML parser finds a `script` tag, it knows that the tasks in this script might alter the page's render tree, so the browser pauses its DOM construction to let the script finish what it wants to do. Once it's done, the browser will resume DOM construction from where the HTML parser left off. Moving script calls to the end of the page and making them asynchronous helps with perceived performance by optimizing your critical rendering path and eliminating those render-blocking issues.

If you make a call to a JavaScript file rather than inlining the script within your HTML, your user's browser needs to go request that file from your server (or a third party's server, if it's a resource you're calling from another site). This could add tens to thousands of milliseconds of wait time before the HTML parser can continue rendering the DOM. However, you can indicate to the browser that this script doesn't need to be executed right away, and therefore shouldn't block content rendering, by adding the `async` tag to your script:

```
<script src="main.js" async></script>
```

This allows the browser to continue to construct the DOM and will execute the script once it's downloaded and ready.

When it comes to asynchronous scripts, there are some "gotchas" to look out for. As you implement asynchronous scripts that load new content, be sure to watch out for how this affects the user experience.

Anything that loads late and affects page layout can cause content to shift, surprising the user; build in placeholders to make sure the page looks and feels stable as it loads.

Note that the asynchronous attribute load order is not guaranteed, which can cause dependency problems. Depending upon the content, you may also consider building in a loading indicator while content is being called asynchronously so that your users understand there are pieces of information missing. Also note that asynchronously loaded content may not play nicely with bookmarks, back buttons, and search engines; keep this in mind as you optimize the critical rendering path and the user experience.

Third-party content like ads, social sharing buttons, and other widgets can be a performance hit on any site. You should already be loading these asynchronously, and ensure that these externally hosted resources are not a single point of failure for your site. Third-party scripts can add a lot of overhead in terms of page weight, but they're also a performance problem because they require an additional DNS lookup and connection since they live off your site. You also won't have control over caching for third-party resources.

Try to eliminate as many third-party scripts as possible. The fewer requests you have, the better your page performance can be. Attempt to combine and condense scripts; you can often do so by replicating, optimizing, and then hosting a third party's script on your own site. Try to replace social sharing scripts with simple links. Routinely assess the value of having a third-party resource called on your page: does the performance hit outweigh the benefit of whatever that resource provides to your users?

In terms of script performance, watch your waterfall charts to make sure that your JavaScript files are loading after your other content and not blocking other downloads or rendering important pieces of the page. Scripts that load ads, social sharing, and other auxiliary content should definitely not block the loading or rendering of other content on the page.

MINIFICATION AND GZIP

See all the whitespace, unnecessary semicolons, and leading zeros in your stylesheets? How about all of those unneeded spaces, newlines, and tabs in your JavaScript files? It's time to *minify* these assets by removing unnecessary characters from the code before they are seen by your end user. Minification results in smaller file sizes, which is great for improving the performance of your site.

You can use command-line tools for minifying your code, or online tools like CSSMinifier.com (*http://cssminifier.com/*) and JSCompress .com (*http://jscompress.com/*). As shown in Figure 4-8, I pasted my site's CSS file into the tool on CSSMinifier.com and it output minified, optimized, and shorter CSS for me to implement on my site. The output was 15% smaller than the original file.

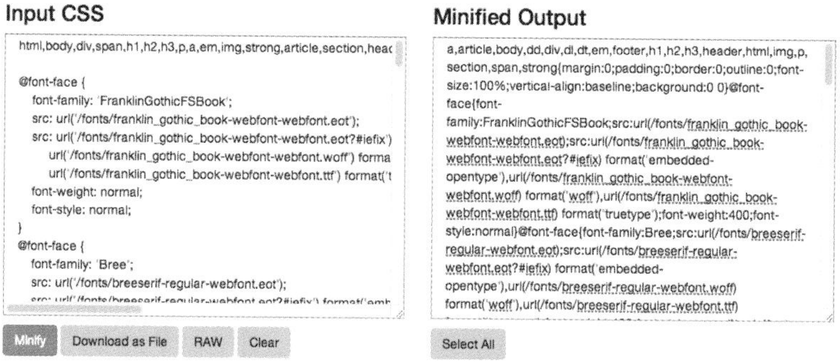

Figure 4-8. In this example, I pasted my site's CSS file into the tool on CSSMinifier.com and it output minified, optimized, and shorter CSS for me to implement on my site.

You'll notice that when you inspect a site's minified CSS it can be hard to find where in the file a particular style is set, as the minified version has everything on one line. Be sure to save a copy of your original, unminified assets, as they'll be significantly easier for you to read and edit in the future than the minified versions. On your site, use the minified versions only, so that your users will download the smallest files possible.

An additional way to compress these text files is to run them through gzip. gzip is a software application used to compress files based on an algorithm. gzip's algorithm finds similar strings within a text file and replaces those strings to make the overall file size smaller. Browsers understand how to decode these replaced strings and will display the content correctly to the user.

To implement gzip compression, you need to enable it on your web server. How to do this depends on your server type:

- Apache: Use mod_deflate (*http://bit.ly/1ttY0BG*).
- NGINX: Use ngx_http_gzip_module (*http://bit.ly/1x6VsYF*).
- IIS: Configure HTTP compression (*http://bit.ly/1ttXYts*).

gzip is great for all kinds of text files like stylesheets, HTML, JavaScript, and fonts. The only exception to this is WOFF font files, which come with built-in compression.

CACHING ASSETS

Caching is critical for your site's performance; assets that are cached do not need to be requested again from your server, saving a request. Caching works by sharing information with a user's browser so it can determine whether to display the previously downloaded (cached) file from disk, or request the asset again from the server.

This information is communicated in an HTTP header, which is the core part of any request sent back and forth between a browser and your server. HTTP headers include lots of additional information like a browser's user agent, cookie information, the type of encoding used, the language the content is in, and more. There are two kinds of caching parameters that can be included in a response header:

- Those that set the time period during which a browser can use its cached asset without checking to see if there's a new one available from your server (Expires and Cache-Control: max-age)
- Those that tell the browser information about the asset's version so it can compare its cached version to the one that lives on the server (Last-Modified and ETag)

You should set one of Expires or Cache-Control: max-age (not both), and one of Last-Modified or ETag (not both), for all cacheable assets. Expires is more widely supported than Cache-Control: max-age. Last-Modified is always a date, and Etag is any value that uniquely identifies the version of the asset, such as a file version number.

All static assets (CSS files, JavaScript files, images, PDFs, fonts, etc.) should be cached.

- When using `Expires`, set the expiration up to one year in the future. Don't set it to more than one year in the future, as that would violate the RFC guidelines.

- Set `Last-Modified` to the date on which the asset was last changed.

If you happen to know when a file is going to change and you'd like to set a shorter expiration, you can do so, though a minimum of one month is still best practice. Alternatively, you could change the URL reference to the asset, which will break the cache and force the user's browser to fetch a new version.

For a guide on enabling caching with an Apache server, read the Apache Caching Guide (*http://httpd.apache.org/docs/2.2/caching.html*). For a NGINX server, read NGINX Content Caching (*http://nginx.com/ resources/admin-guide/caching/*).

Between load order, minification, and caching, you have a lot of levers to play with as you optimize your site's assets for an excellent and fast user experience. Each of these techniques becomes even more important as you implement it for mobile users who are on poorer network connections, especially if you are choosing to display different content for different types of devices or screen sizes. In the next chapter, we'll cover how to deliberately load content for smaller screens and how to create a high-performing and positive user experience for your mobile users.

[5]

Responsive Web Design

Mobile is no longer "the future." As mentioned in Chapter 1, handsets are the primary Internet access method (*http://slidesha.re/eW8wQ9*) for a vast number of global Internet users. People are primarily using handsets to access the Internet, and these devices present their own unique set of challenges. Between the tremendous amount of latency on mobile networks (see "Mobile Networks") and hardware challenges like WiFi signal strength and battery power (see "Mobile Hardware"), it's more important than ever that we design and develop sites that are as high performing and efficient as possible. We need to aim for no unnecessary overhead for our users and optimize for perceived performance on all screen sizes.

The challenge with responsive web design sites is that it can be very easy to accidentally deliver unnecessary content like too-large images or unused CSS and JavaScript. Because the process of creating a responsively designed site can often include *adding* markup and functionality to optimize your layout and content for smaller screens, it's no surprise that many sites deliver the same page weight or additional page weight to mobile devices without the designers and developers even realizing it.

Many creators of responsive sites are already going above and beyond in their decision-making process: reflowing content, choosing to hide or show various elements, making smart decisions about hierarachy, and more. We need to build an additional step into this responsive web design workflow: ensuring that we are delivering only the necessary content in terms of *page weight and requests,* not just information architecture.

Guy Podjarny found (*http://bit.ly/1tBv6cT*) that the majority of responsively designed sites are currently delivering roughly the same page weight to small and large screens. But it doesn't have to be this way:

responsive web design is not inherently bad for performance, and we can be smart about what we deliver to our users. By being intentional in your approach to designing a responsive site and deliberate with what kinds of assets you require your users to download, you can build an excellent user experience that performs well regardless of screen size.

Deliberately Loading Content

Because we so often create a responsive site by *adding* things like more media queries for various screen sizes, it's easy to forget that we may also be adding a ton of extra overhead for our users. This is especially true when a design starts with a desktop version and is then edited to scale down for smaller screens: what happens to those assets that have been optimized for the desktop view? Too often these are left as is; images are always served at the same size (just scaled down visually, through CSS), or fonts continue to be delivered and implemented as they are on desktop. We need to be deliberate with how we load content and ensure we are delivering only the bytes that our user absolutely needs.

IMAGES

Images should be served at the size at which they are displayed on the page to eliminate any unnecessary overhead for your users. In Figure 5-1, we can see a screenshot of Google's home page with Chrome DevTools open. The size at which the Google logo is displayed is smaller than the actual height and width of the logo file.

This means that users are downloading unnecessary bytes, since their browsers downloaded an image that's unnecessarily large for how it's displayed. As you inspect an image in Chrome DevTools, you'll be able to see the height and width of the image as it is displayed on the page as well as the image's "natural" size, which can often be different than the display size (Figure 5-2).

In Figure 5-2, we can see that Google may be sending a retina-sized version of the image to users. Since retina displays cram twice as many pixels into their screens, a designer or developer can send an image twice as large as necessary and scale it down for display in the browser. This technique makes images look crisp on retina displays. Unfortunately, it also means users who aren't using retina displays will download unnecessary image file bytes.

Figure 5-1. In this example, we can see that the size at which the Google logo is displayed is smaller than the actual size of the logo file.

Figure 5-2. Chrome DevTools will tell you how large an image is naturally as well as its actual displayed dimensions on the page.

Inspect the images on your site and see if there are opportunities for serving appropriately sized files. You have a few different ways to tell the browser which image to serve: RESS solutions, CSS media queries, and the new picture specification.

RESS, which stands for *responsive web design with server-side components*, is one option for creating and serving correctly sized images. You can improve performance by choosing which assets to serve to your user on the server side, rather than optimizing them on the client side. Your server can make smart decisions by looking at a user agent string, from which it can guess things like your user's screen size, device capabilities like touch, and more. Tools like Adaptive Images (*http://adaptive-images.com/*) detect your user's screen size and will automatically create, cache, and deliver correctly sized images based on your defined breakpoints (see Figure 5-3). In his book *High Performance Responsive Design* (O'Reilly), Tom Barker outlines a number of RESS techniques and how to implement them.

Figure 5-3. In this example from the Adaptive Images site (*http://adaptive-images.com/*), you can see different pixel widths and heights were generated from a single image with the Adaptive Images tool, as well as the different file sizes of the resulting images.

However, there are a number of downsides to RESS solutions. RESS won't respond to client-size changes (e.g., if a user rotates the device from portrait to landscape). Let's say you're using RESS to send a perfectly resized image to your user's browser. If that user rotates her device and your responsive layout changes, your server won't know to send a new image to fit the new layout. This is why techniques like media queries and the new picture specification tend to be better solutions for responsive images.

There has been a lot of research done to determine which methods are best for displaying a correctly sized image using CSS in a responsive design, thanks in particular to Tim Kadlec (*http://bit.ly/1jqN9gF*) and Cloud Four (*http://bit.ly/1tu0f7X*). However, browsers can do unexpected things as they determine which image(s) to download for your page with CSS, which is why it's important to test your site's performance and ensure that you are asking your users' browsers to download only the necessary resources.

For example, simply setting `display: none` to an element will *not* prevent a browser from downloading the image:

```
<div id="hide">
  <img src="image.jpg" alt="Image" />
</div>

/* Seriously, don't do this.
   Browsers will still download the image. */

@media (max-width: 600px) {
  #hide {
    display: none;
  }
}
```

The same goes for applying `display: none` to an element with a `background-image`; the image will still be downloaded:

```
<div id="hide"></div>

/* Again, don't do this.
   Browsers will still download the image. */

#hide {
  background: url(image.jpg);
}

@media (max-width: 600px) {
  #hide {
    display: none;
  }
}
```

Instead, if you want to hide an image from displaying with CSS in a responsive design, you can try hiding the *parent* element of the element with a `background-image`:

```
<div id="parent">
  <div></div>
</div>

/* Hide the parent element;
   Browsers will not download the image. */

#parent div {
  background: url(image.jpg);
}
```

```
@media (max-width: 600px) {
  #parent {
    display: none;
  }
}
```

Alternatively, you could apply different media queries to tell the browser which `background-image` is appropriate to download at which screen size. A browser will download an image when it matches a media query:

```
<div id="match"></div>

@media (min-width: 601px) {
  #match {
    background: url(big.jpg);
  }
}

@media (max-width: 600px) {
  #match {
    background: url(small.jpg);
  }
}
```

Note that if media queries overlap, older browsers will download both images.

But what about serving up retina images with CSS? We can ensure that only the retina version is downloaded for most browsers by using a media query to serve the retina version:

```
<div id="match"></div>

#match {
  background: url(regular.png);
}

@media (-webkit-min-device-pixel-ratio: 1.5),
  (min--moz-device-pixel-ratio: 1.5),
  (-o-min-device-pixel-ratio: 3/2),
  (min-device-pixel-ratio: 1.5) {
    #match {
      background: url(retina.png);
    }
}
```

Devices running Android 2.x that have a device pixel ratio equal to or above 1.5 will unfortunately download both versions of the image (*regular.png* as well as *retina.png*), but as Kadlec notes in his article (*http://bit.ly/1jqN9gF*), it's unlikely that you will encounter a retina device running Android 2.x.

Your best bet for displaying a correctly sized picture in modern browsers is to take advantage of the picture element in HTML. picture is currently supported in Chrome 38, Firefox 33, and Opera 25, and is a part of the new picture specification (*http://bit.ly/1tu0v6R*). This new specification allows you to tell the browser which image file to download and when, and it includes a fallback for browsers that don't support the picture element.

Here's a simple example of the picture element that uses a media query to determine which image file to download. The first source to match, top to bottom, is the resource that gets picked for the browser to download:

```
<picture>
  <source media="(min-width: 800px)" srcset="big.png">
  <source media="(min-width: 400px)" srcset="small.png">
  <img src="small.png" alt="Description">
</picture>
```

Check out how amazing this is. Not only are we able to match media attributes to tell the browser which image file to download, but we also have a low-resolution image that will be downloaded by browsers that don't support the picture element. Picturefill (*http://scottjehl.github.io/picturefill/*) is a polyfill that enables support for the picture element in browsers that don't currently support it, so you can start using picture today! A good rule of thumb here is that all the images defined in the same picture element should be able to be described with the same alt attribute.

You can use the picture element to serve retina images when applicable, too!

```
<picture>
  <source media="(min-width: 800px)"
    srcset="big.png 1x, big-hd.png 2x">
  <source media="(min-width: 600px)"
    srcset="medium.png 1x, medium-hd.png 2x">
  <img src="small.png" srcset="small-hd.png 2x"
    alt="Description">
</picture>
```

In this example, srcset tells the browser which image to choose at different pixel densities. Again, we're saving overhead for our users by being precise and telling the browser exactly which single image file is the right one to retrieve and display.

One additional superpower of the picture element is the type attribute:

```
<picture>
  <source type="image/svg+xml" srcset="pic.svg">
  <img src="pic.png" alt="Description">
</picture>
```

We can tell our user's browser to ignore an image source unless it recognizes the contents of the type attribute. In this example, browsers that recognize SVG will download the SVG file, and the rest will download the fallback PNG. Again, we're able to tell the browser exactly which single image file is the right one to download and display, saving our user from unnecessary page weight overhead.

But what about fluid designs? Or what if you just have a handful of different image sizes, and want your user's browser to choose the most appropriate resource without listing specific viewport sizes or screen resolutions? The picture specification can help with these, too, using the sizes attribute. sizes follows this syntax:

```
sizes="[media query] [length],
       [media query] [length],
       etc...
       [default length]"
```

Each media query in the sizes attribute will relate to a length that the image will be displayed on the page, *relative to the viewport size*. So if you have a length of 33.3vw, the browser understands that the image will be displayed at 33% of the viewport width. If you have a length of 100vw, the browser understands that the image will be displayed at 100% of the viewport width. This math helps the browser choose which image will be most appropriate to retrieve and show to your user.

sizes is smart because it will look through each media query to see which applies before figuring out the correct image to download. In this example, we can tell the browser that at larger screens, the image will be shown at 33% of the viewport, but the default width of the image is 100% of the viewport:

```
sizes="(min-width: 1000px) 33.3vw,
       100vw"
```

The browser looks in the srcset list of images to see their dimensions. We can tell the browser the width of each image in our list with the syntax image.jpg 360w, where image.jpg is the path to the image file and 360w indicates that this image is 360 px wide:

```
<img srcset="small.jpg 400w,
       medium.jpg 800w,
       big.jpg 1600w"
     sizes="(min-width: 1000px) 33.3vw,
       100vw"
     src="small.jpg"
     alt="Description">
```

With this list of images in srcset and list of display widths in sizes, browsers can pick the best image to fetch and display to your user based on media query and viewport size. This comes in handy when you use a content management system, too; allow your CMS to generate the sources and markup for your image. This way, a CMS user has to upload only one version and not worry about how it will be displayed at different screen sizes. Note that, as demonstrated in this example, you can use the new picture specification without using the picture element!

You can use all of the pieces of this new specification in concert to give your user's browser a ton of power in choosing which image should be downloaded and displayed. You'll be able to choose to serve differently cropped images at different screen sizes, as well as retina-optimized images for high-pixel-density devices, and you can give the browser the power to choose the right image for the job based on media query. All of this is excellent for performance.

FONTS

Font files can add a huge amount of overhead to your site because they require additional requests and increase page weight. As discussed in "Optimizing Web Fonts," there are several ways of optimizing your font files to ensure they are as high performing as possible. One additional consideration you can make in your responsive design is to load your custom font file only on larger screens. This is something we do at Etsy, as we would rather save our users from downloading the extra font file overhead if they're on a mobile device.

To do this, set your normal fallback fonts on your content. Then use a media query to only apply your web font to content at a large breakpoint:

```
@font-face {
  font-family: 'FontName';
  src: url('fontname.woff') format('woff');
}

body {
  font-family: Georgia, serif;
}

@media (min-width: 1000px) {
  body {
    font-family: 'FontName', Georgia, serif;
  }
}
```

This will download and apply the font file only if the user's device matches the media query. All browsers (except Internet Explorer 8 and lower) are smart about downloading a font file only if it applies. Internet Explorer 8 and lower will download all `@font-face` files referenced in a page's CSS file, even if they aren't used on the page.

Approaches

While you'll make many decisions about how to create your site's responsive web design during the actual design and development process, it's important to take a beat before you begin any work to consider your overall approach and how it will impact performance. Building performance into project documentation, taking the time to look at your site from a mobile-first perspective, and figuring out how you're going to measure the performance of your site across media queries will help you to create a speedy, responsively designed site.

PROJECT DOCUMENTATION

If possible, incorporate performance into your project documentation for any project (not just responsive web designs!). For a responsive site, you'll want to benchmark and continue to measure the same standard performance metrics like total page weight, total page load time, and perceived performance using the Speed Index. But you'll also want to be able to set goals for devices and media queries, not just an average overall page using your design.

As we'll discuss in "Approach New Designs with a Performance Budget," there are ways to make compromises on site speed as you develop. By setting a performance budget, you'll be able to make concessions as you balance aesthetics and performance. For any responsive web design, you'll be making these same concessions; maybe you'll want to serve a large image at a particular media query that puts you over your budget, so you'll decide to not deliver extra font weights to make up the time. Table 5-1 outlines an example performance budget for a responsive web design.

TABLE 5-1. Example responsive web design budget

MEASURE	GOAL	NOTES
Total page load time	2 seconds	For all breakpoints
Total page weight	500 KB	min-width: 900 px
Total page weight	300 KB	max-width: 640 px
Speed Index	1,000	For all breakpoints

Set some expectations within your project documentation about how you expect to avoid unnecessary page weight or requests to any device. In addition, make it clear that you will be measuring these things for each media query or screen size and what your goals are, as in Table 5-1. These kinds of budgets can get a bit fuzzy. For example, what happens if you rotate a device and it switches between budgets? It's essential to have a baseline indicating the importance of performance to set expectations for those who are working on the project. Remember that this will benefit not just your mobile users, but your desktop users as well.

MOBILE FIRST

A mobile-first approach to designing any site will help you in so many areas. It will prompt you to:

- Ask critical questions up front ("What is the core purpose of this page?").
- Identify the most important functionality and content for your users.
- Establish design patterns and how they will change across screen sizes.
- Think about your site from an accessibility perspective ("How accessible will this be for people on slower connections or less capable devices?").

By starting with a mobile-first approach, you can attempt to avoid the square peg/round hole mentality that many designers and developers fall into when they try to reshape a desktop experience for mobile devices. You can progressively enhance your site by adding functionality, incorporating more powerful animations and styles, and taking advantage of newer devices' capabilities, all while keeping track of performance implications as you add on.

The mobile experience shouldn't be bare-bones. It should be a deliberate experience; designers and developers should use the benefits of, and be cognizant of the limitations for, each platform their site will be rendered on. Mobile isn't just an add-on to desktop, and desktop isn't just an add-on to mobile. Content parity doesn't mean that each platform's experience should be identical. We should be designing and developing with our users' needs in mind.

A mobile-first approach forces you to ask these important questions about core user needs early and will help you with the performance of your site. An experience with intention about your users will help you focus on what kinds of assets are being delivered to them. An approach in which you make hard decisions about functionality and content hierarchy at small screen sizes will help you keep your total page weight and number of requests down. A site that starts with the most important content and assets, rather than tacking on media queries to handle smaller screen sizes, will be a huge help in keeping your performance under control.

For your responsive site, consider your smallest screen sizes first. Reorder your CSS to deliver small screen styles first, and use progressive enhancement to add content and capabilities as screen sizes get larger. Deliver correctly sized assets, ensure there's no scrolling jank, and make the page's core functionality interactive as quickly as possible. From there, you can make decisions about how to share larger assets on larger screens, reflow content in your hierarchy, and continue to be deliberate about performance in your overall user experience.

MEASURE EVERYTHING

In Chapter 6, we'll cover how to continue to measure your performance as you iterate and test your designs. You'll use all of these tactics on a responsively designed site, just as you would any other site. But there are some additional considerations for measuring a responsive web design.

Primarily, you need to ensure that only the appropriate content is being loaded at each breakpoint. Don't join the other 72% of websites (*http:// bit.ly/1tBv6cT*) that are serving up the same size responsive design site across screen sizes.

If you're able to, implement automated tests that measure the total page weight for each of your chosen breakpoints. Tom Barker included an excellent chapter on continuous web performance testing in his book *High Performance Responsive Design*, which outlines how to implement Phantom JS tests that measure each breakpoint's performance, including YSlow score and total page weight.

You can also test this manually. Emulate a device using Chrome DevTools and use the Resources panel to see which image size is being downloaded for that device. Here is an example set of media queries in which I choose to serve a different image based on breakpoint:

```
@media (min-width: 601px) {
  section {
    background: url(big.png);
  }
}

@media (max-width: 600px) {
  section {
    background: url(small.png);
  }
}
```

I want to make sure not only that the correct image is downloaded for a particular device size, but that *both* images aren't downloaded. I used Chrome DevTools with caching disabled to emulate a Google Nexus 10 that would match the larger media query (Figure 5-4), and a Google Nexus 4 that would match the smaller media query (Figure 5-5).

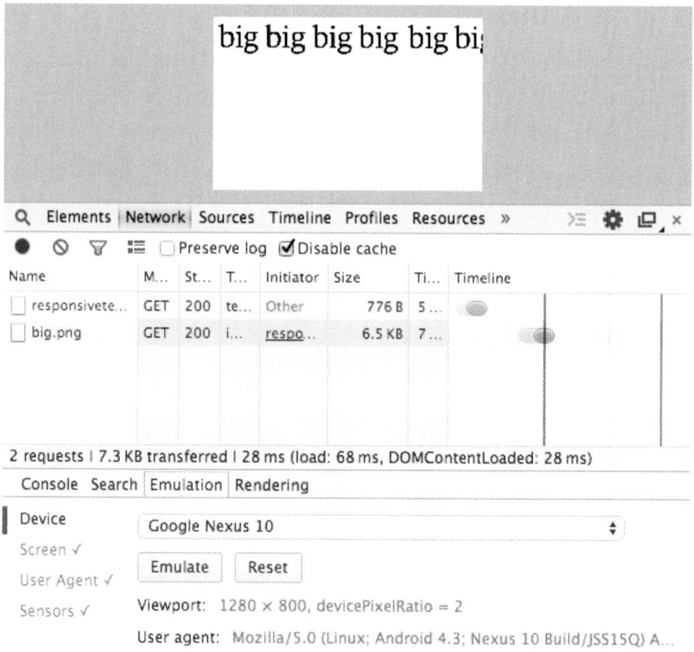

Figure 5-4. In this example, I emulated a Google Nexus 10 to see which image would be downloaded. In the Network panel, we can see that big.png was called.

Each emulated device correctly downloaded only the image that was needed. We can also see the total page size transferred: 7.3 KB for the larger device, and 2.9 KB for the smaller device. Continue to check on the resources and total page weight being delivered to each breakpoint determined in your project plans to ensure that you're meeting your goals.

For measuring total page load time and Speed Index at each break-point, check out WebPagetest's drop-downs for browser (Figure 5-6) and connection speed (Figure 5-7).

The Dulles, Virginia, WebPagetest location includes a number of mobile browsers in the Browser drop-down. This testing location includes physical devices, like the iPhone 4 and the Nexus 5, on which you can test.

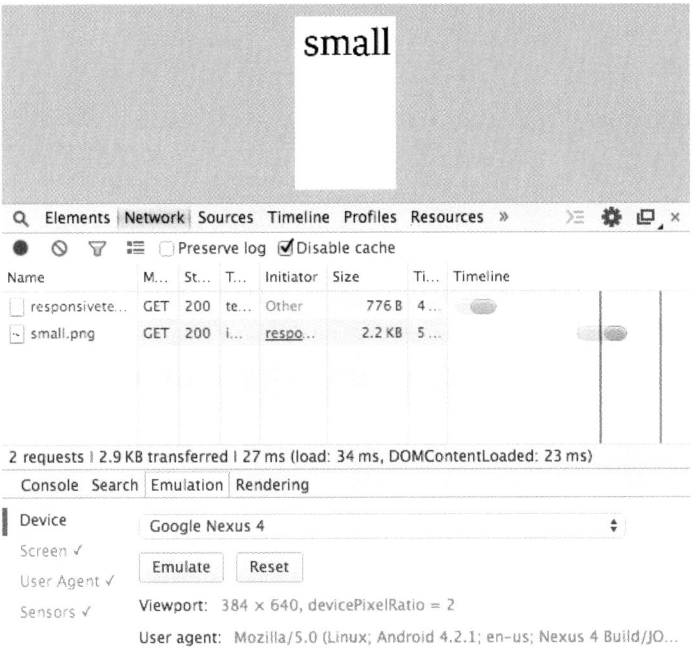

small

Name	M...	St...	T...	Initiator	Size	Ti...	Timeline
responsivete...	GET	200	te...	Other	776 B	4...	
small.png	GET	200	i...	respo...	2.2 KB	5...	

2 requests | 2.9 KB transferred | 27 ms (load: 34 ms, DOMContentLoaded: 23 ms)

Console Search Emulation Rendering

Device — Google Nexus 4

Screen ✓
User Agent ✓   Emulate   Reset
Sensors ✓

Viewport: 384 × 640, devicePixelRatio = 2

User agent: Mozilla/5.0 (Linux; Android 4.2.1; en–us; Nexus 4 Build/JO...

Figure 5-5. After switching the emulator to the Google Nexus 4 and refreshing the page, we can see that small.png was called instead of big.png.

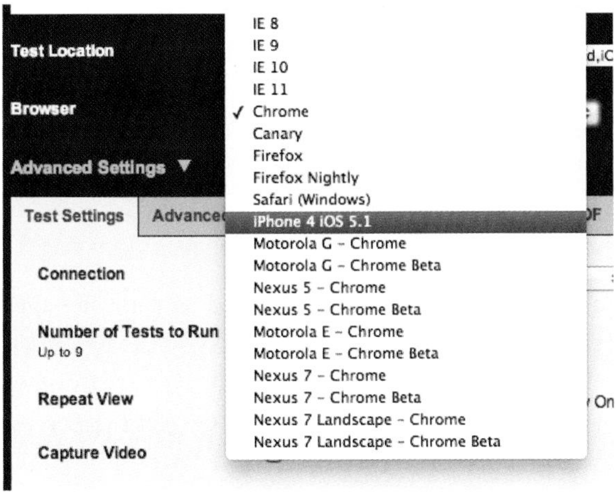

Figure 5-6. You can choose from an assortment of mobile browsers in your WebPagetest run.

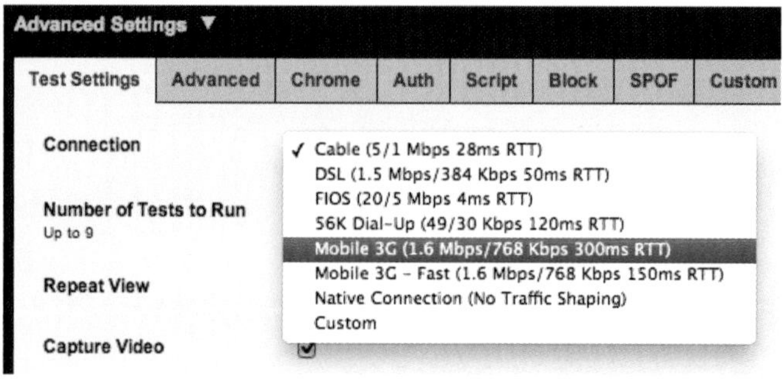

Figure 5-7. You can choose from an assortment of emulated connection speeds in your WebPagetest run.

The different connections listed in the Connections drop-down are created using traffic shaping. This means Chrome DevTools will emulate what a user may experience on this type of connection, but the results will be more consistent across tests because the test is actually happening on WiFi.

Compare the results for each breakpoint to make sure that your total page load time and Speed Index meets or beats the goal outlined in your project documentation.

All of the other techniques in this book will also help you optimize your responsive web design for performance. As you design your responsive site, be deliberate about which assets are downloaded by your users. Develop a performance budget at each breakpoint and use a mobile-first approach when designing and developing the site. Be sure to also check out Tom Barker's book, *High Performance Responsive Design*, for more in-depth details on optimizing both the backend and frontend of your responsively designed website for performance.

As always, measuring performance as you work and as your site ages will help you keep page load time under control. In the next chapter, we'll dive into tools and routines for checking in on the performance of your site to help you get a holistic view of your user experience over time.

[6]

Measuring and Iterating on Performance

Benchmarks are not just critical to understanding the state of your user experience today, but they will also help you pinpoint what contributes to performance changes over time. Routine checks on various page speed metrics like total page load time, total page weight, and Speed Index for perceived performance for your major pages will enable you to see if things get slower on your site (and hopefully, why). Table 6-1 outlines the major tools you can use for benchmarking your site's performance, many of which we'll cover in this chapter.

TABLE 6-1. Benchmarking overview

TOOL	TYPE	BENCHMARK	TIMING
YSlow	Browser plug-in	Overall grade, recommendations	As you develop, then once every quarter
Chrome DevTools	Browser plug-in	Recommendations, waterfall chart, frames per second	As you develop, then once every quarter
WebPagetest	Sythentic testing	Overall grade, recommendations, waterfall chart, Speed Index	Every time you make a large change or experiment
Catchpoint, Gomez, wpt-script, etc.	Sythentic testing (trending)	Trends in your site's performance over time	Monthly
Google Analytics, mPulse, Glimpse, etc.	Real user monitoring	Median load time for various audience demographics	Weekly

As sites age and change, there are plenty of opportunities for both improvements and degradations in performance; it's imperative to keep an eye on these metrics using browser plug-ins, synthetic tests, and real user monitoring.

Browser Tools

To begin to see how well your site performs with basic page load time measurements (Chapter 2), test your pages with browser plug-ins as you develop. Tools like YSlow and Chrome DevTools will help you see how your site stacks up against the key principles of performance optimization.

YSLOW

As mentioned in "Page Weight," YSlow (*https://developer.yahoo.com/ yslow/*) is an excellent way for you to check on your resources' total file sizes. YSlow is a browser plug-in available for Firefox, Opera, Chrome, and Safari; via the command line; and as a bookmarklet. In addition to inspecting the file size of different resources on your page, you can use YSlow to get basic recommendations to improve your page load time (Figure 6-1).

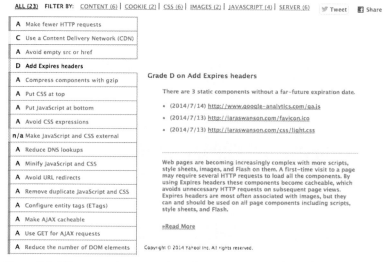

Figure 6-1. YSlow can give you web performance suggestions about your page for things like load order, compression, and caching.

Take a look at YSlow's recommendations for your page. In this case, I've selected its recommendation to add Expires headers to see which files this applies to. I can use this recommendation to spot which resources I need to add caching rules for very easily; in this case, I can ignore the part about caching the Google Analytics script, as it's served by a third party (Google) and the caching rules are out of my hands.

[NOTE]

When reviewing any tool's automated recommendations, remember that you know your site better than anyone. You may see some recommendations that don't quite work with your setup; maybe you know that the way you have optimized your site creates the best user experience for your users, maybe the suggestions apply to third-party scripts that you have no control over, or maybe you know that a certain suggestion wouldn't work for your team's development workflow. Definitely read through all the recommendations and see if they will work for you, but don't worry if the suggestions don't 100% apply. Web performance is rarely one-size-fits-all.

YSlow will give you an overall performance score, which you can aim to improve over time (Figure 6-2). Keep track of your score and regularly check in with it as you iterate on your site's design, content, backend, and so on, and make sure you're staying up-to-date with performance improvements. You can compare this score and set of recommendations to PageSpeed Insights (*https://developers.google.com/speed/pagespeed/insights/*), Google's online web performance analysis tool, as well.

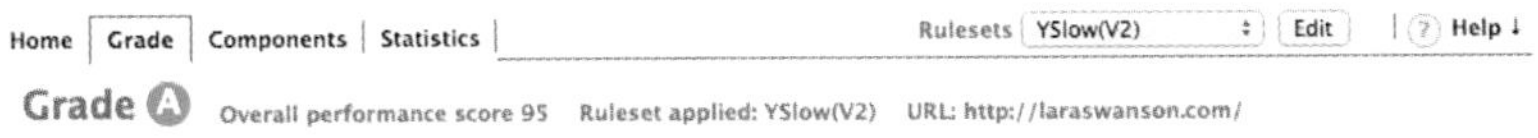

Home | Grade | Components | Statistics | Rulesets | YSlow(V2)   ÷ | Edit | | ? Help ↓

Grade Ⓐ   Overall performance score 95   Ruleset applied: YSlow(V2)   URL: http://laraswanson.com/

Figure 6-2. YSlow will grade your page's web performance, which you should regularly check as your site ages and recommendations change.

Check in with YSlow as you develop a new page, as you make changes to your existing site, or every three months if things are stable. Compare the before and after of your performance grades and recommendations.

CHROME DEVTOOLS

For further optimization, open Chrome DevTools and run a Web Page Performance Audit. DevTools will analyze your page and give you basic web performance improvement tips (Figure 6-3). There are some overlaps between all of the browser plug-ins mentioned here; you'll need to take a look at the recommendations in Chrome DevTools just like in the other plug-ins to be sure the recommendations make sense for your site.

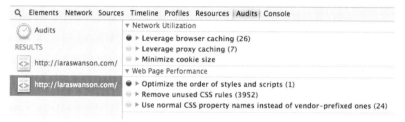

Figure 6-3. Chrome DevTools can run an audit on your page and give you basic web performance tips to speed things up.

After checking out the basic recommendations that DevTools offers, inspect the Network tab (Figure 6-4). This tab shows you a timeline of resource requests on the page that occur while DevTools is open, helping you gather waterfall information as you work on your site.

Figure 6-4. The Chrome DevTools Network tab shows you a timeline of resource requests while DevTools is open, helping you gather waterfall information as you work.

The Network tab is really handy to help you see how the critical path is affected, what resources are taking too long to load, and what kind of latency each request experiences. You can also see cookie information, sort by the duration it takes for resources to load or their latency, and filter by type of request. Poke around the Network tab to make sure that you have a healthy critical rendering path and that there aren't any requests that are taking a tremendously long time to fully load.

We can also use Chrome DevTools to help identify jank. Turn on the FPS (frames per second) meter in DevTools using the Rendering tools window (Figure 6-5) to see which areas of a page trigger a drop in frames per second as you scroll through your site, which is an indicator of poor perceived performance.

Figure 6-5. Chrome DevTools can help you detect which areas of your page trigger jank with the FPS meter.

At Etsy, we found that one of our pages triggered jank when a user scrolled down the page. The team used this FPS meter to help isolate the problem area (in our case, excessive box-shadow on some elements was triggering the jank) so we could make a fix and eliminate the jank on scroll. The team found that fixing the issue had a statistically significant positive impact on engagement metrics. You should run your site through Chrome DevTool's audit recommendations, Network tab, and Rendering tools as you develop a new design or feature, and then once every quarter thereafter.

Now that you've run your site through various browser plug-ins, completed implementation of their suggestions, and spot-checked the site's timeline and frames per second, it's time to get an even more realistic set of performance benchmarks using more browsers and locations.

Synthetic Testing

After you've run your site through browser plug-ins, it's helpful to get a sense of how your site performs outside the comfort of your own browser and geographic location. Synthetic performance tools help you get a better sense of how your pages load by using a third party's testing location and device; you can see how your site performs on various platforms across the world.

Use synthetic tests to get baseline performance metrics for your pages as you iterate and optimize your site's design. Synthetic testing won't necessarily represent what your users are *actually* experiencing when they visit your site (real user monitoring is best for this), but it'll give you a better idea than simply testing in your own browser.

WebPagetest (*http://www.webpagetest.org/*) is a very popular, well-documented, robust synthetic testing solution for performance. You can gain plenty of insight into how your site performs by running tests using WebPagetest (Figure 6-6).

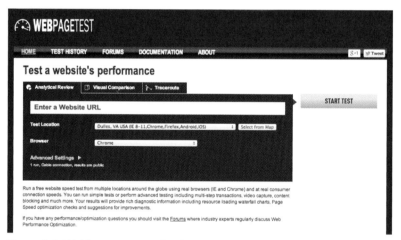

Figure 6-6. WebPagetest provides free speed tests from a variety of browsers and locations around the world.

Running a test on WebPagetest with the default settings will send your page through one first view and one repeat view so you can compare differences in page load time when assets have been cached. The test defaults to a cable connection. You can also choose additional runs under the Advanced Settings (Figure 6-7). I recommend choosing five runs; WebPagetest will select the median first view and median repeat view for result analysis.

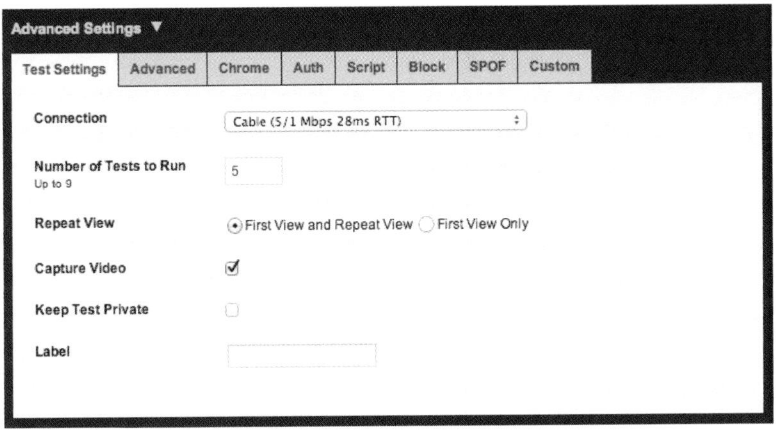

Figure 6-7. WebPagetest's Advanced Settings allow you to choose additional runs, a different kind of connection, and plenty of additional test nuances like the ability to disable JavaScript or have a particular host fail.

WebPagetest will save these results for up to one year, so you can compare your tests to previous results as you begin to improve your site's page load time. If you create an account with WebPagetest, you'll be able to see your tests separate from everyone else's. Also, you can host a private instance (*http://bit.ly/1sHfmre*) of WebPagetest yourself! The added benefits of a private instance include the ability to test a development (nonlive) site, which can be great for incorporating performance into your design and development workflow. You can also automate tests (*https://github.com/etsy/wpt-script*) using a private instance to save yourself some time.

WebPagetest provides page performance recommendations, similar to PageSpeed and YSlow. Choose the Performance Review link at the top of your test to see the details of the test results (Figure 6-8) and your potential page load time savings.

WEBPAGETEST

HOME   TEST RESULT   TEST HISTORY   FORUMS   DOCUMENTATION   ABOUT   8+1 Tweet

Web Page Performance Test for
laraswanson.com/

From: Dulles, VA - Chrome - Cable
7/13/2014 7:43:31 PM

Need help improving?

A	A	A	A	F	F	X
First Byte Time	Keep-alive Enabled	Compress Transfer	Compress Images	Progressive JPEGs	Cache static content	Effective use of CDN

Summary   Details   Performance Review   Content Breakdown   Domains   Screen Shot

Full Optimization Checklist

	Keep-Alive 100%	GZip 100%	Compress Img 99%	Progressive 53%	Cache Static 58%	CDN Detected 72%
http://laraswanson.com/						
1: laraswanson.com - /	✓	✓				
2: laraswanson.com - light.css	✓	✓			✗	
3: laraswanson.com - er_book.png	✓	✓			✗	✗
4: laraswanson.com - lara4.jpg	✓	✓			✓	✗
5: www.google-analytics.com - ga.js	✓	✓				✓
6: laraswanson.com...regular-webfont.woff	✓	✓			✗	✗
7: www.youtube.com - v653j60ALIw	✓	✓				
8: laraswanson.com...webfont-webfont.woff	✓	✓			✗	✗
9: www.youtube.com - 0bRLtJHoOpI	✓	✓				
10: www.youtube.com - RtpVZ50zJlc	✓	✓				
11: player.vimeo.com - 95555576		✓				
12: www.google-analytics.com - __utm.gif	✓					
13: www.google-analytics.com - __utm.gif	✓					
14: s.ytimg.com - w...-webp-vfl_lwTCJ.css	✓	✓				
15: s.ytimg.com - w...player-vflxpaQmw.js	✓	✓			✓	✓
16: s.ytimg.com - h...-en_US-vflMtarS5.js	✓	✓			✓	✓
17: f.vimeocdn.com - player.css	✓	✓			✓	✓
18: f.vimeocdn.com - player.js	✓	✓			✓	✓
19: f.vimeocdn.com - proxy.html	✓	✓			✓	✓

Figure 6-8. WebPagetest provides grades for various performance metrics as well as recommendations on how to improve your page's load time.

In addition to monitoring WebPagetest's Performance Review and your scores for things like First Byte Time and Compress Images, inspect your waterfalls. When looking at a waterfall, identify requests that are taking a significantly long time to load, like in Figure 6-9. These could be flukes, which is why it's good to run multiple tests at once and look at the median result. But they could also indicate issues with file size or content blocking.

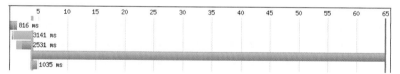

Figure 6-9. When looking at the waterfall for your page within WebPagetest, spot requests that are taking a significantly long time to load.

See what you can do to create nice, short waterfalls on your page. Also look at WebPagetest's Speed Index score. As mentioned in "Critical Rendering Path," Speed Index is the average time at which visible parts of the page are displayed. It will help you benchmark the perceived performance of your page, since it will tell you how quickly the "above the fold" content is populated for your users.

WebPagetest creates a chart that displays visual progress over time when you compare two WebPagetest runs. In Figure 6-10, we can see that the Bing test result was more visually complete faster than Google early on, but the rest of the Google page in this test appeared more quickly thereafter.

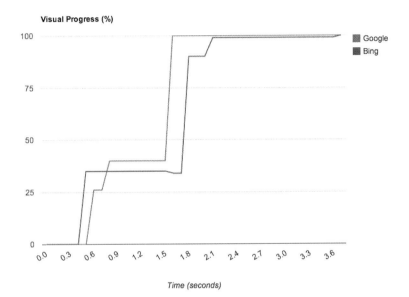

Figure 6-10. WebPagetest's Speed Index score indicates the average time at which visible parts of a page are displayed. You can see a chart representing visual progress over time when you run a comparison between two WebPagetest runs.

In Figure 6-10, the Google Speed Index score was 1228 and Bing's was 1393. The smaller the Speed Index score, the better. Be sure to benchmark your own page's Speed Index score and measure it over time as the site changes, as this is an excellent indicator of the perceived performance of your page.

Be sure to also benchmark your time to first byte, how long it takes for your page to become visually complete, and the time it takes to fully load the page using WebPagetest. Compare WebPagetests results from different browsers and locations to see how each of these metrics changes. Look for outliers in long load times or cases where the critical path may be blocked (read more in "Critical Rendering Path").

As you iterate on a design or make performance improvements on your site, use WebPagetest to measure the before and after results. Be sure to use WebPagetests's filmstrip view and videos for comparisons of how your page loads as you change it over time; also use WebPagetest every time you make a large change to your site or run an experiment.

Synthetic tests like WebPagetest are excellent benchmarking tools as you improve the performance of your site, and for monitoring changes to your site over time and how they impact page load time and perceived performance. Once you get comfortable with benchmarking and iterating on these performance basics, it's time to implement real user monitoring to see what your users are truly experiencing daily on your site.

Real User Monitoring

Real user monitoring (RUM) captures web traffic to your site so you can analyze how long your pages *actually* take to load for your visitors. Unlike synthetic tests, which give you single data points from automated services, real user monitoring tools can give you information about the actual problems your users may experience with your site.

There are plenty of real user monitoring tools out there, ranging in pricing, features, and coverage for your site. Google Analytics (*http:// www.google.com/analytics/*), mPulse (*http://www.soasta.com/products/mpulse/*), and Glimpse (*http://bit.ly/1sHftD3*) are all examples of real user monitoring tools you can compare to see what might work for you and your site.

After choosing a real user monitoring tool, identify your site's major pages to see how they perform for your users over time. The home page, top landing pages, any kind of checkout flow, and other high-traffic, important areas of your site should be included in your main reports. As you look at your users' load time for these pages, segment the data in a few different ways to get a more holistic picture of your end user experience:

- Geographic location (near/far from a datacenter, areas where your main audience lives)

- Network type (cellular, WiFi, etc.)

- Median as well as 95th percentile total page load time

Why 95th Percentile?

The 95th percentile metric is another way to illustrate the performance pain points on your site. The median will give you a general understanding of how long a page might take to load for your user, but the 95th percentile metric is important to ensure that the vast majority of your users have an excellent user experience. The 95th percentile is the slowest 5% of your page views, but 5% is still a notable part of your user base. For RUM, 95th percentile tends to be a measure of how slow your users' network connections are, and slower connections are always going to send the higher percentile through the roof. Note that Google Analytics provides averages for page load time, not percentiles.

Once you have this data, begin to analyze the differences between audience groups, like in Figure 6-11. How different is the median page load time from the 95th percentile? How does the site perform for people in other countries? How about your users on mobile devices? Are there major differences in load time between your top five pages?

Isolate the reasons why these discrepancies exist and figure out what you can do to fix these performance issues. Use the results of real user monitoring tools to gain a better understanding of what your site's user experience truly is for your entire audience, and to help you prioritize performance improvements and fixes.

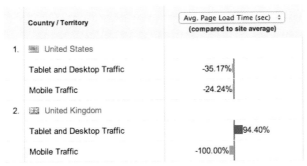

Figure 6-11. Segment your RUM data to find opportunities for performance improvements and get a better understanding of what your users are actually experiencing when they visit your site. In this screenshot from Google Analytics, we can see the differences in load time for traffic on different devices and in different countries.

After benchmarking your site's performance using synthetic testing and real user monitoring, make as many performance improvements as you can until your site's user experience is stable. It can be a challenge to keep site performance stable over time, however, so in the next section we'll walk through how to continue to measure your site's performance after these initial wins to ensure that it stays speedy.

Changes over Time

Sites age. Content gets added. Designs are iterated upon. It's imperative that you routinely run checks on your site's performance to look for any major changes in page weight, total load time, and perceived performance, and for any surprises that could be coming from other areas of your organization.

You're likely not the only person who is working on your site. There could be other designers, developers, and content creators who are contributing new changes that affect things like load order, file sizes, scroll jank, and more. By benchmarking your site's performance and checking in on it with some routine, you'll be able to pinpoint any surprises in performance that arise. Did the home page suddenly double in load time thanks to a new image carousel? Was a marketing script just added to every page on the site? Did a blog post author accidentally upload images that are five times larger than they need to be? Be sure to routinely audit your major pages and find those performance surprises. In Figure 6-12, we can compare average page load time for my site's users over time.

It's also possible that there are no significant changes over time, but rather gradual degradations in performance. These are harder to spot and fix. On larger, more complex sites, you may start to see time to first byte increase, or page load times for the 95th percentile get slower and slower. By routinely benchmarking performance you can compare quarter to quarter, in addition to week to week, which should also help you alert others to less obvious changes in performance over time. The more aware you and the team are about performance, the more equipped you'll be to troubleshoot and balance out normal site aging implications.

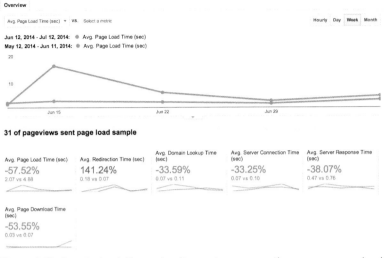

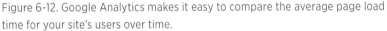

Figure 6-12. Google Analytics makes it easy to compare the average page load time for your site's users over time.

Routinely check on your images, as we walked through in "Image Planning and Iterating." Schedule routine checks on the cleanliness of your sprites, image formats, and compression. Make sure that any new images uploaded to your site are automatically compressed and that you're serving them at the right size. At the same time, check on the page weight for your site's top five pages. If any of them have increased by a significant amount, isolate the reason and either fix the regression or find other places to improve performance on the page. If you have a performance budget, you can often work within this budget and find other ways to fix increases in page load time (read more in "Approach New Designs with a Performance Budget"). But all of this work depends on you regularly checking in on the performance health of your site and documenting it over time in an easily comparable way.

Some companies use an internal wiki page to manually track performance changes over time. Other companies create dashboards and alerts using data from third parties like performance monitoring tools or WebPagetest's self-hosted option. It's helpful to document both performance metrics as well as any reasons *why* performance changed; you can see which kinds of site changes have huge impacts on performance over time (redesigns, new ad or marketing scripts) and which are minor (such as small changes in content or images).

Etsy's Q1 2014 Site Performance Report

There was a small increase in both median and 95th percentile load times over the last three months across the board, with a larger jump on the home page. We are currently running a few experiments on the home page, one of which is significantly slower than other variants, which is bringing up the 95th percentile. While we understand that this may skew test results, we want to get preliminary results from the experiment before we spend engineering effort on optimizing this variant.

This kind of log will help you educate those around you to understand how their work affects the overall end user experience. It'll also help you go to bat when you need to defend your decision to weigh aesthetics versus performance, as we'll discuss in Chapter 7. By benchmarking each week's performance data and why it's changed, you'll empower everyone within your organization to make smart decisions in their daily design or development workflow.

One additional item to watch over time is your competitors' page load time. If you're able, run tests and benchmark how their sites perform over time. This can give you data about how much of a priority performance is for them, and also help you understand what aspects of the user experience they are working on over time. Spot a major performance change and investigate it: did they add new marketing tracking, incorporate a better hero image, or implement web fonts that indicate new branding? This kind of data can help you defend the importance of your own site's performance over time to the Very Important People within your organization.

Keeping an eye on performance can be a meticulous task, so you should try to automate this data gathering and create alerts when major changes happen. Build dashboards with the data that you have and share them within your organization. If you have performance budgets or service-level agreements for a performance metric, be sure to indicate these on your graphs so you can see how much room you have or how much work there is to do. Dashboards for performance over time will be incredibly helpful for watching those slow performance degradations that are harder to spot.

Automatically alerting on performance regressions and wins will also save you a ton of time. If one of your main pages increases in week-over-week total page load time, you should be notified in a convenient way. Trigger emails or an alert that gives you the context of what the old performance benchmark was versus now, and make it easy to figure out exactly when those numbers changed. If possible, alert those individuals responsible for an area of the site if its performance changes. You can do this for wins, too; celebrate with an alert when there's a huge improvement in performance and thank those responsible.

Over time, you will affect the page load time of your site by making both aesthetic and performance improvements. Be sure to measure all of these changes and how they impact your business metrics with A/B tests. You could be making an intentional performance improvement, or you may have a design change that will negatively impact performance; A/B tests are great for tracking all of this! Benchmarking performance as it changes over time, especially when you can directly attribute it to work being done on your site, will empower you and others to make smart decisions about aesthetics and performance. In the next chapter, we will examine how experiments are great for optimizing your overall user experience, and look at some challenges you'll face when balancing design and performance.

[7]

Weighing Aesthetics and Performance

Your site's overall user experience is made up of so many different pieces: look and feel, accessibility, information architecture, usability, and more. Performance is just one piece of the overall user experience. We can use performance to boost other areas of the site. If you cut down on page weight, you'll make it more accessible to users on limited bandwidth. If you improve perceived performance, the site will *feel* better.

However, speeding up your site can have costs. You'll lose development time that you could be spending working on other areas of the user experience. You may find yourself making sacrifices in other areas of the experience (like the look and feel) in order to improve performance. In this chapter, we wrestle with when to make tough calls about doing performance work, what it can cost you, and when it's worth it.

Finding the Balance

You now know how browsers request, retrieve, and display content to your users. You understand how different image formats work and what they're best used for. You've thought about the semantics and repurposability of design patterns in your HTML and CSS, and you understand the importance of tweaking load order for the critical path. You *get* performance. Now it's time to leverage your new skill set.

Performance is closely linked to aesthetics. Frontend architect and consultant Harry Roberts notes, "it's not about how nice something looks, it's about how nicely it works, how it feels. There's no point designing a nice, shiny, beautiful UI if it's going to take 20 seconds to end up on a user's device. They'll have left before they even got to see it."

If it were as easy as always following the same patterns and guidelines, maybe more people would be doing performance work today. But unfortunately, it takes tough decision making to do performance well. Thankfully, having all this knowledge about how the Web works will help you make the right choices for you and your site. By understanding the way that JPEGs find areas of a picture to compress, you can make a call about the export quality of that image and whether you should even use the JPEG format. By understanding character subsetting and how the number of requests on a page affects performance, you can make decisions about how many font weights you should call on a page.

Sometimes you'll make choices that favor performance; other times, you'll make choices that favor aesthetics. The key is using all the information available to you to make the right decision for you and your site.

At the outset of a project, you may find yourself weighing tough choices like those in Table 7-1.

TABLE 7-1. Example aesthetic and performance considerations

QUESTION	AESTHETIC CONSIDERATION	PERFORMANCE CONSIDERATION
Can I put a large hero image at the top of every page?	Eye-catching, represents the brand well	This could be a really large file, and we want to minimize page weight.
Should I @font-face three display weights and a text weight?	Lots of flexibility in typography	We want to minimize requests and page weight.
Will I put a carousel on the home page?	Showcases a lot of different content	We want to minimize requests and page weight (especially for content that the user may not even see).
How will I demonstrate how our product works?	Could use video or animated GIF	Videos and GIFs can be pretty heavy.

The answers may differ every time, due to new context like the codebase you're working with, deadlines, the team members with whom you're working and their skill sets, the look and feel, and more. Table 7-2 shows example decisions made after weighing these considerations.

TABLE 7-2. Example site decisions

QUESTION	DECISION
Can I put a large hero image at the top of every page?	Yes. We'll make sure that few colors are used in the hero, and it's compressed correctly.
Should I @font-face three display weights and a text weight?	We'll use two display weights and a system font for the body content.
Will I put a carousel on the home page?	No, the incremental benefit to our UX is not worth the extra requests and page weight.
How will I demonstrate how our product works?	We'll self-host a video that asynchronously loads.

While doing work for their client Fasetto, Roberts and brand designer Naomi Atkinson made tough calls about when to sacrifice aesthetics and performance. In one case, they wanted to showcase how simple Fasetto was to use, and decided to go with animated GIFs. But, knowing that GIFs (especially animated ones!) can be very heavy, why did they choose to go this route?

- Atkinson was already skilled at making animated GIFs. Roberts and Atkinson recognized that they needed to account for familiarity with tools and development cost as well as balancing aesthetics and performance when making this decision.

- Replacing GIFs with CSS animations would have inflated the size of the CSS, which they were aiming to deliver in a single request. Roberts was focused on the critical path of the site, and wanted to allow the GIFs to render progressively during the page load rather than as part of the critical path.

- Atkinson was able to limit the color palettes of the GIFs to leverage this file format's compression algorithms. She focused on striking a balance between appearance and file size.

The resulting animated GIFs landed at just under 35 KB, with one outlier at 90 KB. Atkinson and Roberts relied on their performance knowledge to make smart design decisions and deliver the best possible user experience for their client.

When you encounter these choices, weigh:

- The performance difference
  - How many requests would it add or remove?
  - How much page weight would it add or remove?
  - How would perceived performance be impacted?
- The aesthetics difference
  - How would this affect the brand?
  - How would this impact existing design patterns?
  - How would this change affect the overall user experience?
- The operational cost
  - How maintainable is this solution? Will this make the site's codebase cleaner?
  - Is this team able to contribute to this solution?
  - How much time will this take to build?
  - Is there a benefit to the team in learning this technique? Can it be leveraged on other projects?

It can be very challenging to find a happy medium when you're weighing this many varied and sometimes oppositional aspects. However, you're now equipped with an understanding of performance, and you can use this knowledge to make good decisions for your end users. There are some additional techniques you can use to make these choices easier: incorporate performance into your daily workflow to diminish its development cost, approach all new designs with a performance budget, and continually experiment with designs to learn about how your decisions are paying off.

Make Performance Part of Your Workflow

One way to minimize the operational cost of performance work is to incorporate it into your daily workflow by implementing tools and developing a routine of benchmarking performance.

There are a variety of tools mentioned throughout this book that you can incorporate into your daily development workflow:

- Automate image compression as new images are added to your site.

- Use an image resizing service and caching by breakpoint so you don't need to manually create a new image for every screen size.

- Document copy-and-pasteable design patterns in a style guide for easy reuse.

- Check your page weight and critical path using browser plug-ins.

By making performance work part of your daily routine and automating as much as possible, you'll be able to minimize the operational costs of this work over time. Your familiarity with tools will increase, the habits you create will allow you to optimize even faster, and you'll have more time to work on new things and teach others how to do performance right.

Your long-term routine should include performance as well. Continually benchmark improvements and any resulting performance gains as part of your project cycle so you can defend the cost of performance work in the future. Find opportunities to repurpose existing design patterns and document them. As your users grow up, so does modern browser technology; routinely check in on your browser-specific stylesheets, hacks, and other outdated techniques to see what you can clean up. All of this work will minimize the operational costs of performance work over time and allow you to find more ways to balance aesthetics and performance.

Approach New Designs with a Performance Budget

One key to making decisions when weighing aesthetics and page speed is understanding what wiggle room you have. By creating a performance budget early on, you can make performance sacrifices in one area of a page and make up for them in another. In Table 7-3 I've illustrated a few measurable performance goals for a site.

TABLE 7-3. Example performance budget

MEASURE	MAXIMUM	TOOL	NOTES
Total page load time	2 seconds	WebPagetest, median from five runs on 3G	All pages
Total page load time	2 seconds	Real user monitoring tool, median across geographies	All pages
Total page weight	800 KB	WebPagetest	All pages
Speed Index	1,000	WebPagetest using Dulles location in Chrome on 3G	All pages except home page
Speed Index	600	WebPagetest using Dulles location in Chrome on 3G	Home page

You can favor aesthetics in one area and favor performance in another by defining your budget up front. That way, it's not always about making choices that favor page speed; you have an opportunity to favor more complex graphics, for example, if you can find page speed wins elsewhere that keep you within your budget. You can call a few more font weights because you found equivalent savings by removing some image requests. You can negotiate killing a marketing tracking script in order to add a better hero image. By routinely measuring how your site performs against your goals, you can continue to find that balance.

To decide on what your performance goals will be, you can conduct a competitive analysis. See how your competitors are performing and make sure your budget is well below their results. You can also use industry standards for your budget: aim for two seconds or less total page time, as you know that's how fast users expect sites to load.

Iterate upon your budget as you start getting better at performance and as industry standards change. Continue to push yourself and your team to make the site even faster. If you have a responsively designed site, determine a budget for your breakpoints as well, like we did in Table 5-1.

Your outlined performance goals should always be measureable. Be sure to detail the specific number to beat, the tool you'll use to measure it, as well as any details of what or whom you're measuring. Read more about how to measure performance in Chapter 6, and make it easy for anyone on your team to learn about this budget and measure his or her work against it.

Experiment on Designs with Performance in Mind

The most important superpower you have when doing performance work is the ability to measure its effects. You can measure *everything*: how much time did it take you to make this improvement? How did it impact bounce rate? Was it worth the aesthetic sacrifice? Better yet, can you compare two options side-by-side and measure what's better for your users (*A/B testing*)?

Learn how your decisions are paying off by measuring them. If there's one thing I've learned from years of doing A/B testing, it's that I will always be surprised. As developers and designers who have gotten to know our user base, we often jump to conclusions and assume we know what's best for the user experience, rather than measuring how our users are really responding to our choices. If you haven't been running experiments, it's time to start.

In an A/B test, you can run two different versions of a page on your site at the same time to different segments of your users. The number of users who see the test will determine how long your site needs to run. By running the two versions concurrently and measuring how your users behave after seeing the test, you can learn how your decisions about aesthetics and performance impact the overall user experience. Read more about how to set up and run experiments in this primer on A/B testing (*http://alistapart.com/article/a-primer-on-a-b-testing/*).

I've been surprised by the results of performance experiments. For example, there have been times when users react more positively to the *addition* of font weights, even though it slowed down the page. However, many performance experiments have confirmed for me the power of page speed as part of the overall user experience, like when we added 160 KB of hidden images to a page and saw a 12% increase in bounce rate from our users on mobile devices. If you have a tough decision to make about a design, run an experiment to see how your users really react.

Too often, the "aesthetics versus performance" mentality results in a "designers versus developers" culture. But developers don't have to be in a silo making performance improvements, and designers don't have to be on an island making aesthetic improvements. The team can and should work together with a common goal: a great user experience. Harry Roberts, who has teamed up with many designers and clients to make beautiful websites that are optimized for performance, says,

"Now instead of a design team who wants beautiful, an engineering team who wants fast, and a product owner who just wants delivery, you have a whole team who all want to make beautiful, fast products, quickly."

It's always going to take a human brain to make these kinds of decisions. Rather than a "versus" mentality, opt for a "What's best for our users?" mentality. Sometimes you may find yourself ignoring the outcome of an experiment because it's not best for your users. For example, what if a performance gain results in poorer security for your users? How often do you see a site being a little sleazy in its user experience (like making it all too easy to accidentally spam all your contacts) just to make more revenue? When an outcome of an experiment is better for your business metrics, gut-check it to make sure it's still great for your users.

At the end of the day, a great user experience is what we're aiming for. In his blog post "Page Weight Matters" (*http://blog.chriszacharias.com/page-weight-matters*) Chris Zacharias outlines an experiment that he ran as a developer at YouTube. The video watch page had climbed to 1.2 MB of page weight with dozens of requests, and Zacharias decided to prototype a version of the page with limited functionality that loaded significantly faster. He launched this prototype, dubbed "Feather," as an opt-in experience to a fraction of YouTube's traffic.

The results, as Zacharias says, were "baffling." The measured load times had increased for these users, even though the page was significantly smaller. The reason? Zacharias wrote, "entire populations of people simply could not use YouTube because it took too long to see anything. Under Feather, despite it taking over two minutes to get to the first frame of video, watching a video actually became a real possibility. Over the week, word of Feather had spread in these areas and our numbers were completely skewed as a result. Large numbers of people who were previously unable to use YouTube before were suddenly able to."

This is why we do performance work, and why we measure it. Finding that balance between aesthetics and performance requires considering the entire user experience and testing to make sure what your gut says is right. However, it can be tough to get an entire organization on board with this work. It can be difficult to convince upper management that the cost of the time spent on this work can benefit the business as well as your end users. It can also be difficult to get the rest of a design and development team on board with doing this kind of work. In the next chapter, we'll walk through what you can do to change the culture of your organization to focus on performance.

[8]

Changing Culture at Your Organization

The largest hurdle to creating and maintaining stellar site performance is the culture of your organization. No matter the size or type of team, it can be a challenge to educate, incentivize, and empower those around you. Performance more often comes down to a cultural challenge, rather than simply a technical one.

It is rare to have a culture of performance in which everyone at an organization values the impact that performance has on the user experience. Often, there are performance cops or janitors at a company who take it upon themselves to improve site speed. Sometimes, companies will dedicate infrastructure team resources toward performance improvements. There should absolutely be performance champions at your organization (in fact, you're probably one of them!). However, limiting the responsibility of performance to a small group of people will make it nearly impossible to keep the site's speed under control, particularly as the site ages, changes, and is worked on by new people.

It's important to recognize when a problem needs technical solutions, when it needs cultural solutions, and when it needs both. Many of the chapters in this book cover technical solutions for performance, but the cultural solutions covered here will help you leverage these technical solutions' impact and make sure it lasts.

Performance Cops and Janitors

Performance improvements often begin as one person's voice within a company culture. You start to notice how other sites are making optimizations and improving their user experience through tweaks to perceived performance or total page load time. Then you start measuring how your competitors' sites fare in WebPagetest and comparing your site's performance to theirs. After beginning to learn about many of the easy performance wins that you could implement on your site, you start crafting improvements with little effort and tons of gains.

These are the individuals who often start out as performance cops or janitors. Cleaning up after other designers and developers becomes a routine chore for these individuals; sometimes they've taken this responsibility on themselves, or sometimes they were assigned these responsibilities. Either way, this road leads to burnout.

As time marches on, so many things will continue to create performance challenges for even the most stable site:

- New performance techniques emerge, like the recent implementation of `picture`.

- The site's hardware, brand, and code age.

- New designers and/or developers are hired.

- Existing designers and/or developers with great performance habits leave.

- Browsers continue to evolve.

- Web standards evolve, such as HTTP/2, which eradicates some existing performance constraints.

Having a dedicated team of people responsible for keeping track of these kinds of evolutions is important. A performance champion, or a team of performance champions, is an excellent tool for a company to lean on as the Web changes. But the responsibility for maintaining a high-performing site should not solely rest on the shoulders of these individuals. Everyone who works on the site should buy in to the importance of performance and understand what they can do to improve it.

If other designers and developers who shape the site aren't educated on performance, how can they make the best decisions about user experience? How can they weigh the balance between aesthetics and page speed? If they aren't empowered to make improvements, any performance champions will simply be playing cleanup after other people's work. Spending your time cleaning up other people's work (especially when it's preventable) is a one-way ticket to burnout.

A dedicated performance team can focus on:

- Giving lectures, lunch-and-learns, and workshops to educate others about performance

- Celebrating the good work of designers and developers on other teams who improve site speed

- Building tools to surface performance data in others' daily workflows to help them understand how they are directly impacting performance in their current work

- Defining baseline requirements for performance, such as a performance budget for each new project or a maximum page load time across the site

- Learning about emerging technology and new methods of improving performance

- Communicating publicly about changes in site performance and recent experiments and learnings, as shown in Figure 8-1

Figure 8-1. Etsy's performance report details load time for top pages and what changes contributed to the load time each quarter.

Having an individual or team care deeply about performance is important for all of the aforementioned purposes. These champions can stay on top of how performance is being handled sitewide; they can keep an eye on problem areas, look for areas to improve, and raise suggestions to the other people contributing to the site's design and development. But the work to be done to actually improve and maintain performance needs to be owned and shared across your organization, rather than lie with an individual or single team.

Upward Management

Page speed is a relatively intangible problem. Though it's easy to get numbers around it, performance is mostly about perception and feeling. Total load time and frames per second don't easily communicate to people *why* they should care about making improvements; problems that are less tangible like this often need a champion within an organization who comes from a place of power. Very Important People who care about performance will help you dramatically shape your organization's culture.

To emphasize the importance of performance upward, focus on showcasing it both within business metrics and with end user experience. The first angle involves numbers: impact on conversion rate, total revenue, returning visitors. The second angle focuses on helping these VIPs *feel* how slow your site is and empathize with your end users.

IMPACT ON BUSINESS METRICS

There are plenty of studies across the Internet that demonstrate the business metric impact of performance, some of which we discussed in Chapter 1:

- Akamai has reported that 75% of online shoppers who experience an issue such as a site freezing, crashing, taking too long to load, or having a convoluted checkout process will not buy from that site (*http://bit.ly/1ttKKNf*).

- Gomez studied online shopper behavior (*http://bit.ly/1ttKspI*) and found that 88% of online consumers are less likely to return to a site after a bad experience. The same study found that "at peak traffic times, more than 75% of online consumers left for a competitor's site rather than suffer delays."

- Users will return to faster sites, as evidenced in a study by Google (*http://bit.ly/1ttKPR8*) that noted a decrease in searches for users who experienced a site slowdown.

- DoubleClick, a Google ad product, removed one client-side redirect (*http://bit.ly/1ttLjqx*) and saw a 12% increase in click-through rate on mobile devices.

Identify what kinds of numbers your upper management cares about. Is it revenue? Membership? Social media engagement? Once you figure out which metrics matter to them, find and share performance research with them that relates to those particular metrics. Correlate engagement metrics (such as bounce rate, click-through rate, and returning visitors) with revenue and other bottom-line metrics that resonate with this audience. Each organization and its VIPs have defined business drivers to which you can draw parallels from these studies.

If possible, run experiments on your own site to correlate performance improvements to the metrics these folks care about and share them alongside the other public research. While big sites like Amazon and Google can run slow-down experiments to measure the impact that a slower site has on its users, your organization probably won't like the idea of you intentionally slowing down the site just to see what happens. Focus on finding high-impact quick performance wins, like compressing images or implementing better caching.

Make one significant improvement and measure its engagement metric impact. If possible, run an A/B test to compare your audience's behavior in the control to your new, improved variant. If you're able to move the needle on revenue-related metrics like conversion rate, terrific; if not, focus on other engagement metrics like bounces and pages per visit. Tie any statistically significant improvements in your new high-performing version to the metrics that upper management cares about. A lower exit rate, for example, could mean more users choosing you over a competitor or returning to search engine results.

If you're unable to run an A/B test, measure engagement metrics before you make the improvement and again afterward. It won't be scientific, but it'll be the best case you can make to upper management. Read more about measuring the impact of performance improvements in Chapter 6. Share the work you did and the resulting business metric changes with those VIPs to help them understand the impact that performance work can have.

As you make any performance changes, also measure how long it takes you to do so. Design and development hours are a cost for the business, and you'll need to address this as you work on turning VIPs into champions of your cause. Find the quickest and most impactful wins possible to start to emphasize that improving the user experience doesn't have to be a large cost to the business. Translating a specific number of resource and development hours into a revenue win for the business will be your biggest asset in the conversation, and will help you continue to get support as larger and more time-intensive performance work is needed.

Conversations with upper management should include a blend of public research from around the Internet, research that you've done on your own site, as well as the cost of this kind of work to the business. A holistic approach to these conversations should be grounded in an understanding of which engagement metrics and business factors resonate the most with your internal audience.

EXPERIENCING SITE SPEED

Helping upper management understand what your users are experiencing on your site is key. We can talk numbers all day, but getting to the root of how your performance affects your users will require you to focus on your site's user experience. Remember that most people within your organization are probably accessing your site on newer hardware with fast connections and are probably relatively close to your datacenter. How do people around the globe experience your site? How do people experience your site when they're not on a desktop computer?

Run multiple WebPagetests using different locations and devices and compare the results. You can compile all of the results into a single filmstrip view to compare them using this URL structure: *webpagetest. org/video/compare.php?tests=<Test 1 ID>,<Test 2 ID>*...

For example, in Figure 8-2 I ran three separate tests for the *Huffington Post*'s site: one using the Virginia test location using Chrome on a desktop, one using Internet Explorer 8 from the Singapore location, and one using Chrome on an Android phone from the Virginia location. While the overall numbers varied widely for each test and could make a compelling argument for mobile and global performance improvement needs, the filmstrip view really helps you *feel* the difference in user experience.

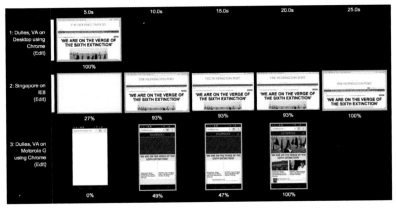

Figure 8-2. WebPagetest provides a filmstrip view as well as video for you to compare tests at the same time. This helps give you a better understanding and feel for the performance of these sites.

Another angle to consider during these conversations is pride. While revenue impact is a great metric you can use to convince upper management that performance should be an important consideration for any designer and developer at your organization, it's not the only tool in your tool belt. Your site likely has competitors. How do their page load times compare?

WebPagetest also allows you to compare multiple URLs before you begin a test for a visual comparison of performance (see Figure 8-3). All of these tests in the Visual Comparison tool will use the Dulles, Virginia, testing location.

Figure 8-3. You can enter multiple URLs into WebPagetest to compare their performance.

Once the tests complete, WebPagetest can show you a filmstrip view of how each page loads over time, as shown in Figure 8-4. You can even export a video of the page loads in tandem; this really helps people *feel* the difference of how the sites are loading. You're able to avoid numbers altogether, instead focusing on gaining an understanding of how your users are *experiencing* your site and your competitor's site in the same time frame.

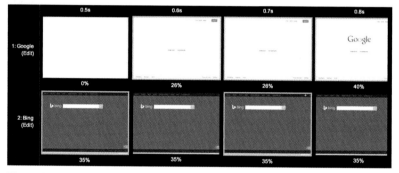

Figure 8-4. Use WebPagetest's filmstrip view and video comparison to gain a better understanding and compare the performance feel of different sites.

Page speed and user experience are not secrets. Any of your competitors can test your site, or run it through performance tools and see how you're stacking up. Remind the Very Important People in your organization that you are being analyzed not just by your users, but by your competitors, too. Be sure that you are outperforming your competitors' sites.

One last way to utilize the filmstrip and video views is to compare the before and after of a performance improvement you make to your site. While measuring the impact that the improvement had on engagement metrics is powerful, it can be equally helpful to document the visual of how differently the site loads, particularly if your improvement helps perceived performance rather than total page load time.

Use these tools during your conversations with upper management to help make the case that everyone at your organization has an impact on the end user experience and should focus on performance as part of their daily work. A site that feels fast requires everyone who affects the user experience to keep performance top-of-mind during their daily workflows.

Working with Other Designers and Developers

Education and empowerment are key to incentivizing the other designers and developers with whom you work to care about performance. The responsibility is on you to continually equip them with the tools that they need as well as the reasons to care about how they impact user experience when they affect your site's performance. While it's true that hammering home the negative consequences of poor performance will help make it clear how important it is, championing and celebrating performance wins is often way more successful in the long run. Help those around you care about delivering an awesome user experience and know how valuable their work is as it impacts performance.

EDUCATING

There are many ways that focusing on performance helps designers and developers. Considering things like semantics and repurposability of what's being built up front saves a ton of design and development time later. The ease of editability increases, and future headaches are prevented when code is cleaner and design patterns can be easily updated across the site at once or repurposed.

Beyond these wins, you'll need to educate others at your organization about how they impact performance in their daily lives. Brown-bag lunch sessions, lectures, and workshops are all excellent ways to communicate to and train people about how they can be better designers and developers by focusing on performance. Consider leading an effort to teach people about topics such as:

- How mobile performance works
- How people can impact performance during the design stage
- How to improve perceived performance

Share slide decks and presentation videos from others about how to design excellent, high-performing user experiences. Education is an ongoing effort; you'll have new hires who are unfamiliar with these techniques, and folks who forget about best practices when they get swamped with other work. Routinely give lunch-and-learns or other informal education about how everyone can have a positive impact on performance.

Develop baselines for your organization as to what's acceptable for page load time. How slow is too slow? Communicate the acceptable page load time threshold to everyone: "We're aiming for one-second total page load time for each page." Alternatively, assess what the best-performing pages on your site are and how fast they load, and use that as a benchmark across the site. Be sure to measure the worst-performing pages that get a lot of traffic on your site and suggest that the entire team focus on getting those as fast as possible. People should be given easy-to-follow guidelines and benchmarks so that it's clear where the wins are and what to aim for.

If you're able to run automated tests to gather performance information for your most important pages, do so. Make sure the team has visibility into when a page's performance gets worse so that you can figure out what changes contributed to the decline and fix them. Set up alerts on worsening performance and share them with other designers and developers so that everyone can learn as the site evolves.

For each new project, develop a performance budget and make sure all designers and developers understand what it means. Educate them about these numbers and how they can weigh aesthetics and speed. Read more about performance budgets in "Approach New Designs with a Performance Budget." Providing baseline guidance and easy-to-understand (and easy-to-measure) metrics for the entire team will empower them to contribute to a stellar user experience.

EMPOWERING

To empower people to make good choices during their daily workflows, figure out how to surface performance data on their current work. At Etsy, we have a toolbar that appears when an Etsy employee is logged in to the site, as shown in Figure 8-5. Designers and developers use this toolbar to understand information about the page they're looking at as they work on the page; it includes visit traffic data, a list of any experiments that are currently being run on the page, and tools to view the mobile version of the page. It also includes performance timing data and an alert whenever the performance times violate our performance service-level agreements.

Figure 8-5. At Etsy, we show a toolbar to employees working on site pages. It surfaces performance timing data and makes it clear when a page has performance problems so that the designer or developer working on the page is alerted to the issue.

Showing performance data in this way is helpful to designers and developers, as it is a constant reminder that performance is part of the user experience. Rather than waiting to see how fast a site is after it's been built, consider ways to routinely empower designers and developers with this knowledge as they're working.

Another way to routinely share this information is to send automated emails if any performance regressions occur across the site. Equipping people with this knowledge *as it happens* is an important step toward empowering people to immediately fix it. Make this kind of performance metric knowledge a part of daily life and workflows so that it feels natural, like it's just part of doing a good job at work.

Once people have the tools and education needed to understand the performance of your site and how they can impact it, they'll begin to feel empowered to improve it. But remember, this is a cultural problem, not a technical one; though there are a lot of technical solutions that can help people improve site speed, you'll need to do extra work to solve the social aspects of performance culture.

One way to change the culture at your organization is to begin to publicize your performance efforts. When I worked at Dyn, I published a summary of how I completed a huge template cleanup and included the performance improvements that resulted. It not only helped educate the readers of Dyn's blog, but it also made the performance win highly visible to all Dyn employees.

When frontend architect and consultant Harry Roberts completed a chunk of performance work for a client, he shared the numbers with them. "They got very, very excited about the numbers, and even began running their own tests on it. Giving them something like this to get into really brought them on board so, from then on in, they cared as much about keeping the numbers down as I did," said Roberts.

Publishing your work and celebrating it is a huge incentive to many designers and developers; showcasing improvements, as I did in Figure 8-6, is a great way to kick-start culture change and encourage others to contribute to performance wins.

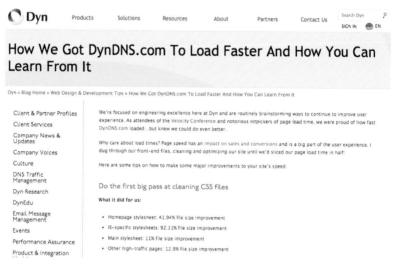

Figure 8-6. After I finished a template cleanup effort across DynDNS.com, I published a summary of how I did it and the performance improvements we saw.

At Etsy, the performance team attempted a different public tactic to effect culture change. In 2011, the team published its first performance report that included an outline of load times for the top pages on the site, which you can see in Figure 8-7. It included some relatively embarrassing metrics, but the performance team realized that it was important to acknowledge the opportunities for performance improvement. They recognized that site speed is not a secret—it can be measured by anyone—and these numbers were important for everyone at Etsy to recognize because they reflected the site's actual user experience.

After publishing the first report, the team responsible for working on the home page realized how embarrassing their numbers were. They worked on improving load time by making some hard decisions about features and how they were designed, weighing the balance between aesthetics and speed. They were able to reduce the home page's load time significantly by the time the next performance report was released, as shown in Figure 8-8.

Etsy News Blog

Tech Update: Faster and Faster

Search

Search the Blog   Search

Other Editions

Australia Edition   Nederlandse Blog
Blog Français   Deutscher Blog
UK Edition   Seller Handbook
The Etsy Blog

Stay In Touch

Photo by JBCPhotography

Story by bethwalker
Published on July 08, 2011 in Product Announcements

Of all the awesome new features we delight in rolling out to our members, one of the most satisfying features to deliver is speed. In the past year we've made targeted improvements to convos, search, and relisting performance, and we've greatly improved page delivery times to our members outside the U.S. We gain more than warm fuzzies with these improvements. Studies have shown that slow pages lead to less engaged visitors – they click fewer links, read fewer pages, and make fewer purchases. And just as you fiend for your iced latte to go, site performance is becoming increasingly important as more of our members access Etsy through mobile devices and networks.

Seth

We have already taken our commitment to performance to the next level. We have been gathering every-which-way measurements around site performance, and we will be kicking off more projects to improve performance across the board. Continuing in our spirit of

Figure 8-7. Etsy published its first performance report in 2011, intentionally including some embarrassingly long page load times.

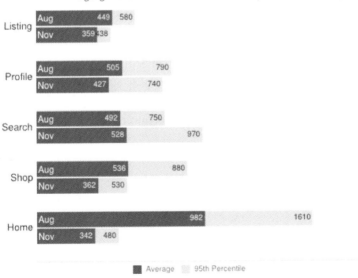

Figure 8-8. In its second performance report, Etsy showcased huge improvements in home page load time.

Publicly acknowledging how your site is performing will make people feel accountable, and will also make them want to help. Designers and developers generally want to help contribute to a common, positive cause, and making this cause public will help kick-start this feeling.

Another way to help kick-start the culture shift is to make it very easy for the team to feel productive when making performance improvements. Find all of the low-hanging fruit across the site—that is, work that could be easily picked up by another designer or developer—and start documenting it. File tickets or start a list that people can quickly reference. Here are some examples of easy performance wins you can share:

- Clean up and normalize existing button styles across the site, and document where all the different buttons live so people can pick them off one by one.

- Isolate suspect chunks of CSS that are likely no longer needed in your stylesheet and ask someone to verify that they're no longer needed, then have folks clean them out.

- Find large images used on the site and list them so that someone can re-export them, compress them, or find other ways to optimize their file size.

For each ticket or item on your list, include enough detail about the fix needed so that someone picking it up can immediately work on the solution. Keep each piece of work bite-sized, no more than a few hours each. If a fix takes more than a few hours, ask the designer or developer to simply document the progress so that another person can pick it up again in the future. It should be intuitive and easy for other designers and developers to begin contributing to making your site faster.

As others begin contributing to the overall performance of your site, the most important thing you can do is celebrate their work. For every bite-sized performance improvement, thank the contributor and publicize their work internally, like in Figure 8-9.

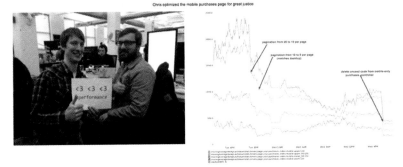

Figure 8-9. The performance team at Etsy maintains a dashboard celebrating people on other teams who contribute to performance improvements. We include their photo, a graph showing the performance improvement, and a brief description of their solution.

At Etsy, we maintain an internal dashboard where we can celebrate "performance heroes": people on other teams who contribute fixes and improvements to our site's page load time and perceived performance. We routinely update it to showcase the creative efforts of the people with whom we work, highlighting any relevant graphs that illustrate the performance improvement and a description of the solution they implemented. We'll also send out an email to the other designers and developers at Etsy to indicate we've updated the dashboard so that everyone can chime in and high-five the person who improved the site.

Performance is truly everyone's responsibility. Anyone who affects the user experience of a site has a relationship to how it performs. While it's possible for you to single-handedly build and maintain an incredibly fast experience, you'd be constantly fighting an uphill battle when other contributors touch the site and make changes, or as the Web continues to evolve. Educate and empower everyone around you to understand how they can improve performance, and how their choices affect the end user experience. Performance truly is about making a cultural shift, not just a technological one; build performance champions within your organization so that you can create the best user experience possible for your site.

Web performance work is as fulfilling as it is challenging. You have the power to go and create an excellent experience for your users. Find those performance wins, whether they're implementing new caching rules, optimizing images, or creating repurposable design patterns. Empower those with whom you work to be performance champions. Strive for the best possible user experience, striking a balance between aesthetics and speed. With a focus on performance, everyone wins.

[*Index*]

About the Author

Lara Callender Hogan is the Senior Engineering Manager of the Performance team at Etsy. Lara previously managed Etsy's Mobile Web Engineering team. Before joining Etsy, Lara was a User Experience Manager and self-taught frontend developer at a number of startups. She's been certified as an EMT, owned her own photography business, and co-founded an LGBT wedding website. She also believes it's important to celebrate career achievements with donuts.

Colophon

The animal on the cover of *Designing for Performance* is a tufted coquette (*Lophornis ornatus*), a tiny hummingbird that breeds in eastern Venezuela, Trinidad, Guiana, and northern Brazil.

Also known as the splendid coquette, this hummingbird is so tiny that it can easily be confused with a large bee as it moves from flower to flower. Its red beak has a black tip and is short and straight. The female doesn't have very flashy plumage, but the male has striking black-spotted and orange-colored feathers that project from the sides of his neck and an orange head crest.

Hummingbirds in general are quite solitary, so the tufted coquette is mostly found alone or in small groups, as it searches for nectar and small insects to feed on.

Many of the animals on O'Reilly covers are endangered; all of them are important to the world. To learn more about how you can help, go to *animals.oreilly.com*.

The cover image is from Wood's Natural History. The cover fonts are URW Typewriter and Guardian Sans. The text font is Scala Regular; the heading font is Gotham Narrow Medium; and the code font is TheSansMonoCd Regular.

Have it your way.

O'Reilly eBooks

- Lifetime access to the book when you buy through oreilly.com
- Provided in up to four, DRM-free file formats, for use on the devices of your choice: PDF, .epub, Kindle-compatible .mobi, and Android .apk
- Fully searchable, with copy-and-paste, and print functionality
- We also alert you when we've updated the files with corrections and additions.

oreilly.com/ebooks/

Safari Books Online

- Access the contents and quickly search over 7000 books on technology, business, and certification guides
- Learn from expert video tutorials, and explore thousands of hours of video on technology and design topics
- Download whole books or chapters in PDF format, at no extra cost, to print or read on the go
- Early access to books as they're being written
- Interact directly with authors of upcoming books
- Save up to 35% on O'Reilly print books

See the complete Safari Library at safaribooksonline.com

©2014 O'Reilly Media, Inc. O'Reilly logo is a registered trademark of O'Reilly Media, Inc. 14373

Get even more for your money.

Join the O'Reilly Community, and register the O'Reilly books you own. It's free, and you'll get:

- $4.99 ebook upgrade offer
- 40% upgrade offer on O'Reilly print books
- Membership discounts on books and events
- Free lifetime updates to ebooks and videos
- Multiple ebook formats, DRM FREE
- Participation in the O'Reilly community
- Newsletters
- Account management
- 100% Satisfaction Guarantee

Signing up is easy:

1. Go to: oreilly.com/go/register
2. Create an O'Reilly login.
3. Provide your address.
4. Register your books.

Note: English-language books only

To order books online:
oreilly.com/store

For questions about products or an order:
orders@oreilly.com

To sign up to get topic-specific email announcements and/or news about upcoming books, conferences, special offers, and new technologies:
elists@oreilly.com

For technical questions about book content:
booktech@oreilly.com

To submit new book proposals to our editors:
proposals@oreilly.com

O'Reilly books are available in multiple DRM-free ebook formats. For more information:
oreilly.com/ebooks

O'REILLY®

©2014 O'Reilly Media, Inc. O'Reilly logo is a registered trademark of O'Reilly Media, Inc. 14373